Elite • 162

World War II Desert Tactics

Paddy Griffith · Illustrated by Adam Hook

Consultant editor Martin Windrow

First published in Great Britain in 2008 by Osprey Publishing,
Midland House, West Way, Botley, Oxford OX2 0PH, UK
443 Park Avenue South, New York, NY 10016, USA

ISBN: 978 1 84603 290 5

Editor: Martin Windrow
Page layout by Ken Vail Graphic Design, Cambridge, UK
Maps by John Richards
Typeset in Helvetica Neue and ITC New Baskerville
Index by Glyn Sutcliffe
Originated by PPS Grasmere, Leeds, UK
Printed in China through World Print Ltd

08 09 10 11 12   10 9 8 7 6 5 4 3 2 1

A CIP catalogue record for this book is available from the British Library

FOR A CATALOGUE OF ALL BOOKS PUBLISHED BY OSPREY MILITARY AND
AVIATION PLEASE CONTACT:

NORTH AMERICA
Osprey Direct
C/o Random House Distribution Center, 400 Hahn Road, Westminster,
MD 21157
Email: info@ospreydirect.com

ALL OTHER REGIONS
Osprey Direct UK
PO Box 140, Wellingborough, Northants, NN8 2FA, UK
Email: info@ospreydirect.co.uk

Osprey Publishing is supporting the Woodland Trust, the UK's leading
woodland conservation charity, by funding the dedication of trees.

www.ospreypublishing.com

Author's acknowledgements

I am grateful to all who helped me in the preparation of
this book, especially Robert Baldock, Andy Grainger, Paul
Harris, Matthew Hughes, John Ellis, David Fletcher and
Major T.A. Bird DSO, MC, Rifle Brigade, who was at the
'Snipe' action at Alamein. Also to the staffs of the RMA
Sandhurst library, the Imperial War Museum reading room,
the Public Record Office (as it was then called – and in my
opinion still should be), and the Tank Museum, Bovington.
In the last I was honoured to meet Sgt Ron Huggins, who
told me of his experiences in the 10th Hussars at Gazala,
where he was wounded. I am also grateful to John Richards
for his work on the maps, and to Adam Hook for
interpreting the intricacies of the colour plates.

Artist's note

Readers may care to note that the original paintings from
which the colour plates in this book were prepared are
available for private sale. All reproduction copyright
whatsoever is retained by the Publishers. All enquiries
should be addressed to:

Scorpio Gallery,
PO Box 475,
Hailsham,
E.Sussex
BN27 2SL, UK

The Publishers regret that they can enter into no
correspondence upon this matter.

Glossary of abbreviations and terms

AA	Anti-aircraft		RHA	Royal Horse Artillery – in theory a more mobile version
ACV	Armoured Command Vehicle ('Mammoth')			of the field artillery, so more appropriate for use in
AFV	Armoured fighting vehicle			armoured divisions; in practice, in 1940–43 it used
AP	Armour-piercing			the same towing vehicles.
AT	Anti-tank		RTR	Royal Tank Regiment – an organization of 24 active
Bde	Brigade			(and 10 dummy) numbered battalions, of which
Bn	Battalion			18 active (and 4 dummy) battalions served in the desert.
Co, Coy	Company		TD	Tank Destroyer – US category of fighting vehicle and unit
DAK	Deutsches Afrika Korps		VC	Victoria Cross – Britain's supreme award for valour
Div	Division (e.g. Armd = Armoured, Inf = Infantry,			in combat
	Mot = Motorized, Pz = Panzer, German armoured)			
HE	High Explosive		Battalion	In all armies, a unit comprising a headquarters sub-unit
I-tank	British 'infantry' tank: at first the Matilda Mk II, later			and three or four combat companies
	joined by the Valentine and Churchill		Brigade	In the British Army, a formation of three battalions
RA	Royal Artillery		Regiment	In the Italian, German and US armies, a unit of two or
Regt	Regiment			three battalions, equivalent to the British brigade; in the
REME	Royal Electrical & Mechanical Engineers			British Army, a battalion-sized unit of armoured cavalry
				or artillery.

WORLD WAR II DESERT TACTICS

A HARSH AND VAST ARENA

When the British Expeditionary Force retreated through Dunkirk in early June 1940, it abandoned not only all of its guns and vehicles, but also any idea of conducting major operations in north-west Europe for the next four years. Later in the same week, however, the Italians judged it safe to enter the war. New theatres of operations were suddenly opened in the Balkans, East Africa and especially North Africa, which would give the British Army plenty to do until the final capture of Tunis in May 1943. And not just the British, since contingents from all over the world would quickly become engaged in the battle as it ebbed and flowed for three years across a vast swathe of Libya, Egypt, and eventually Tunisia. By the end of these campaigns the combatants in North Africa would include (apart from North Africans themselves) forces from America, Australia, Britain, France, Germany, Greece, India, Italy, New Zealand, Poland and South Africa, not to mention a Jewish brigade, and an AA battery from Hong Kong and Singapore.

The campaign in North Africa was not only highly international: it was also the most technologically advanced of World War II, in the sense that it was the only one to be fought (at least until it reached Tunisia) without the use of horses or mules. It was pure mechanized warfare, and as such

British sun compass. Much of the desert terrain was featureless, but pinpoint accuracy in navigation was essential, and not only for tactical movements: replenishment echelons had to find tanks and guns, and artillery and aircraft had to be directed on to specific targets. The sun compass was an invaluable instrument, because the magnetic compass was useless inside a vehicle made of steel. The sun compass could be mounted just next to the vehicle commander, for constant checking on the march; to use a magnetic compass he would have to stop, dismount and walk some distance away from the vehicle. (Tank Museum collection; author's photo)

Schematic cross section of the terrain of the North African coastal desert where operations took place.

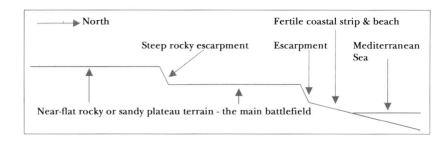

North — Steep rocky escarpment — Escarpment — Fertile coastal strip & beach — Mediterranean Sea

Near-flat rocky or sandy plateau terrain - the main battlefield

it was the long-awaited test for many of the futuristic theories and speculations that had been put forward during the 1920s and 1930s. At first sight the open desert terrain seemed to be 'good tank country' or even 'a tactician's dream', and there was quite a lot of loose talk about how the tanks would sail around effortlessly like warships in the open sea. The tank itself had, after all, originally been conceived as a 'Land Ironclad' (after H.G. Wells' short story of 1903), and it was first developed by the British Admiralty. The analogy was soon elaborated into a whole taxonomy of 'capital tanks', 'cruiser tanks', 'destroyer tanks', 'tank harbours', 'tank marines' and so forth.[1]

Alas for all this optimistic idealism, it soon became apparent that before 1940 very few European soldiers had had the slightest idea of what this terrain was really like – especially not from the point of view of large-scale mechanized warfare. It turned out that the vast, bare landscape fell very far short of a tactician's dream, and for a wide variety of reasons. Its very openness made it notoriously difficult for anyone to find cover, so that entire divisions might sometimes have to form up facing each other in the open, within artillery range, in a way that had not been seen since the middle of the 19th century. The infantry often had to keep its transport miles to the rear to protect it from enemy fire. It was also extremely difficult to navigate accurately, and many are the stories of vehicles being lost for hours on end, sometimes wandering into the enemy's leaguers without either side realizing it. In the summer the mirages could cause multiple distortions of the light that made observation, and range-finding by optical instruments, impossible. The rockier patches might resist the excavation of foxholes unless pneumatic drills or explosives were used; while the heat, the flies and the sandstorms constantly mocked all the normal expectations of 'civilized' warfare.

All participants agreed that whatever it might do for tacticians, this harsh and gigantic arena certainly made for 'a logistician's nightmare'. The main problem with fully mechanized warfare was, of course, that it depended on the internal combustion engine; each engine had a strictly limited mileage, and this was radically reduced when the vehicle had to drive through sandstorms and fields of light grit which permeated the moving parts. An unprecedented effort had to be put into recovery, maintenance and repairs. Fuel consumption was also exceptionally high, which raised particular problems when lines of supply became stretched over many hundreds of miles – there were no civilian filling stations at the roadside, such as had helped the Germans forward in their French campaign. Over most of this theatre of war the railheads

[1] See the exemplary discussions in Paul Harris, *Men, Ideas and Tanks* (Manchester University Press, 1995)

stopped very far short of the front-line fighting. Not even water was available in anything like the quantities required, which meant that great efforts had to be put into carting it over enormous distances, with the normal daily ration per man often falling to as little as half a gallon for all purposes – including keeping the vehicles' radiators topped up. North Africa was such an unforgiving environment – in these and many other ways – that every mile travelled required a mechanical effort equivalent to well over two miles travelled in north-west Europe – and of course, in North Africa there were many more miles to be travelled.

With very few exceptions, formations that entered this theatre suffered an initially very rude awakening. The first to launch an offensive – on foot, for lack of sufficient motor transport – were Marshal Graziani's under-supplied and second-line Italian troops in September 1940. They did not prosper, even before the December counter-attack by the British 7th Armoured, 4th Indian and then 6th Australian Infantry Divisions – all three of which included experienced veterans who had studied desert conditions before the war. However, these British Empire formations were soon replaced by much less desert-aware troops. Equally, when Erwin Rommel made his first bold attack from El Agheila with the *Deutsches Afrika Korps* (DAK) in March 1941, he found that 83 out of 155 of his tanks quickly broke down, mainly for want of 'desertized' oil filters; Panzer Regiment 5 was left with only 25 'runners' for its vital assault on Tobruk on 11 April, which was duly repulsed.

The Germans, however, would soon learn from their mistakes, and the DAK would rapidly establish itself as the outstanding fighting force in North Africa, as well as enjoying the greatest continuity of personnel. After Rommel's irruption into the theatre, the over-stretched British Empire had to keep feeding in formations that were mostly fresh,

1 February 1941, near Derna: Australian infantry carrying up rations and water over typically unforgiving stone-desert; water supply was a constant problem and limiting factor in this theatre. The officer leading them seems to carry a thermos container, and a couple of the Diggers have what look like beer bottles. By this stage in Gen O'Connor's campaign this had become practically a rear area; nevertheless, Derna was starved of motor transport, which had largely been diverted to the mobile spearheads that were just about to win the decisive battle of Beda Fomm hundreds of miles away near Benghazi. (IWM E 1845)

British officers peering into an M4A1 Sherman II, loaded on to an American trailer for road movement. In 1940–41 it was found that the vast distances to be travelled could wear out a tank's running gear before it even arrived on the battlefield. The need for tank transporters became obvious and urgent, but it would be a long time before enough of them became available. This brand new Sherman has just been issued in October 1942 to C Sqn, 3rd Hussars; under magnification the white horse sign and tactical serial '40' on a green rectangle are just visible on the left track guard, identifying 9th Armd Bde and this regiment respectively. The brigade was virtually annihilated while attacking the German AT-gun screen – the 'PAK-front' – on 2 November during the 'Supercharge' phase of Second Alamein. (IWM E 16861)

inexperienced and unacclimatized to desert conditions. They enjoyed an overall numerical and material superiority, but all too few genuine desert veterans. Small-scale exceptions included Gen Koenig's two gnarled French Foreign Legion battalions, who did so well at Bir Hacheim in June 1942, and the Long Range Desert Group, which pioneered operations in the deep desert.[2] Larger contingents which at least had some relevant terrain and climate experience included the Australians who held Tobruk throughout most of 1941, and the South Africans who fought at Sidi Rezegh in November that year.

Nevertheless, in some of these cases there was a certain sacrificial element to their efforts: they were unable to achieve everything of which they should have been capable, because the great bulk of the British Empire forces fighting alongside them tended to be operating well below par. All too many of the latter were consumed in the fire of combat within only a few days of entering it, and were thus brutally prevented from growing and maturing into veteran desert warriors in due time. One of the most shocking examples of this was the 23rd Armd Bde, which arrived at Suez from Britain on 6 July 1942; they had their tanks 'ready for action' (more in theory than in reality) by 17 July, and entered combat at El Mreir on the 22nd. In other words, they had just four days to get used to running their vehicles in Egyptian terrain before they were sent into the attack, when the normally accepted minimum for such acclimatization was at least a month. Apparently their radios were not yet netted, and few of the crews had even been told that the enemy had anti-tank guns capable of penetrating their armour. Thus it should have surprised no one that in the first four hours of battle they lost approximately 110 of their 150 Valentine tanks (or 73 per cent), to mines, AT guns and a Panzer counter-attack.

[2] See Battle Orders 23, *Desert Raiders: Axis & Allied Special Forces 1940–43*

The final, and extremely numerous, arrivals in North Africa would consist of the American Fifth and British First Armies that landed in Operation 'Torch' in November 1942, followed by the large and belated inrush of Axis troops to Tunis in the winter of 1942–43. Very few of these forces, of any nationality, had seen action before, nor had they experienced North African conditions. This only served to confirm the general rule that most of the troops who fought in this theatre were less than ideally prepared for the challenge. This was especially true of most of the quarter of a million Axis troops – equivalent to the numbers captured at Stalingrad – who would surrender when Tunis fell in May.

The multiplicity of British tanks

(A-numbers indicate tanks built to General Staff specifications)

Light tanks (very light but very fast)

Vickers Mk VI: Derived from Carden-Lloyd carrier; armed only with MG

Cruiser tanks (fast but light)

A9/ Cruiser Mk I: Armed with 2-pdr AT gun plus MGs
A10/Mk II: Similar but thicker armour; only 170 built
A13/Mks III & IV: Christie suspension; only 65 plus 270 built
A15/Mk VI 'Crusader': Christie suspension; 5,000 built, some late production with 6-pdr AT gun
US M3 Light ('Stuart'/'Honey'): 37mm AT gun

Infantry (I-) tanks (heavy but slow)

A12/ Mk II 'Matilda': heavy armour, 2-pdr AT gun; 2,987 built
Mk III 'Valentine': derived from A10 & A12, used as hybrid of both Cruiser and I-tanks; inadequate armour for latter role; 8,275 built
A22/'Churchill': heavy armour; 2-pdr, later 6-pdr AT gun; excellent performance in Tunisian hills

'Capital' tanks (combining good speed, armour & firepower)

US M3 Medium ('Grant'): 37mm AT turret gun, 75mm multi-purpose gun in hull sponson, with limited traverse; excessively large 6-man crew
US M4 Medium ('Sherman'): 75mm GP turret gun, heavier armour, mechanically reliable – the best available compromise until 1945

CHRONOLOGY

This is, obviously, only a thumbnail chronology of the major events. Entries in *italics* are approximate dates of appearance in theatre of the first examples of significant new equipment (usually only in small numbers initially, supplementing rather than replacing previous equipment).

1938
Sept   Mobile Division (later British 7th Armd Div) formed in Egypt by Percy Hobart

1940
11 June   Italians declare war: border skirmishes sustained, especially by British 11th Hussars.
13 Sept   Italians invade Egypt
20 Sept   First use of Takoradi air reinforcement route via Nigeria to Egypt
8–11 Dec   Operation 'Compass' launched by Gen O'Connor: battle of Sidi Barrani won by British with much greater ease than had been feared

1941
5–7 Feb   Battle of Beda Fomm completes O'Connor's victory
5 March   First British troops sail for Greece, removing major parts of Western Desert Force

British motor infantry in the pursuit to Enfidaville, mid-April 1943. This photo gives an unusual impression of just how much ground a formation could occupy if it was dispersed as widely as regulations demanded (despite the lack of an enemy air threat by this stage of the campaign). There are more than 20 vehicles in sight, spread over an area perhaps 500 yards square. (Tank Museum 2260/C3)

30 March	Rommel's counter-attack into Cyrenaica pre-empts planned British attack into Tripolitania: British routed, although with few casualties
7 April	Gens O'Connor and Neame captured
10 April	Siege of Tobruk begins, as Rommel presses on to Libya–Egypt frontier
5–12 May	'Tiger' convoy brings tanks through the Mediterranean to Alexandria
15–17 May	Op 'Brevity' – small action on Libya–Egypt frontier
15–17 June	Op 'Battleaxe' – slightly larger British offensive, but no more successful – has important implications for future British tactics
June–July	British campaign against the Vichy French in Syria
5 July	Gen Wavell replaced as C-in-C Middle East by Gen Auchinleck; Gen Cunningham appointed GOC British Eighth Army
25 July–8 Aug	British enter Persia and quell resistance
14–15 Sept	Rommel's 'Midsummer Night's Dream' raid to Sofafi
18 Nov–16 Dec	(but technically to 17 Jan 1942, when Halfaya surrendered): Op 'Crusader' – British achieve initial surprise and eventually win a victory after 4 weeks, rather than the 3 days envisaged. In the process Gen Cunningham replaced by Gen Ritchie as GOC Eighth Army
27 Nov	Final Italian surrender in East Africa ends war in that theatre
10 Dec	Allied garrison of Tobruk relieved
1942	
Early 1942:	*German PzKw III Ausf J (to British, 'Mk III Special'), with thicker armour, long 5cm gun with high penetration up to 1,000 yards*
21 Jan	German counter-offensive at El Agheila pre-empts planned British Op 'Acrobat' into Tripolitania; major British defeat, but again with light casualties
2 Feb	British occupy Gazala line and prepare Op 'Buckshot' to re-take Cyrenaica
May	*British 6-pdr AT gun, effective up to 1,500 yards. British Grant tank (US M3 Medium)), with thicker armour, 37mm AT in turret & multi-purpose 75mm gun in hull sponson*

26 May	Battle of Gazala: Rommel achieves initial surprise, from which British do not recover. Heavy fighting continues until –
20 June	Tobruk captured by the Axis
25 June	Gen Auchinleck takes direct command of Eighth Army from Gen Ritchie
24–27 June	Battle of Mersa Matruh – shameful British retreat in face of inferior enemy numbers demonstrates extent of demoralization
1–26 July	First battle of Alamein – British defensive victory, but no more
13 Aug	Gen Montgomery appointed GOC Eighth Army, and Gen Alexander C-in-C Middle East, to replace Gen Auchinleck in both posts
Aug	*PzKw IV Ausf F2 (to British, 'Mk IV Special'), with thicker armour, long 7.5cm gun with penetration up to 2,000 yards*
13 Sept	Failed amphibious attack on Tobruk
30 Aug–7 Sept	Battle of Alam el Halfa – British defensive victory
Oct	*British Sherman tank (US M4 Medium), with thicker armour, 75mm multi-purpose turret gun*
23 Oct–3 Nov	Second battle of Alamein – British offensive victory
8 Nov	Op 'Torch' landings in French Morocco and Algeria by British First and US Fifth armies, which enter Tunisia from west on 12 Nov.
Nov	*PzKw VI Tiger, with very heavy armour and unrivalled 8.8cm multi-purpose main gun*
1943	
14–25 Feb	Major Axis attacks from Sidi Bou Zid to Kasserine – eventually repulsed
Feb	*German Nebelwerfer 6-barrel barrage rocket launcher*
6 March	New Axis attack repulsed in battle of Medenine
March	*British 17-pdr AT gun, almost equivalent performance to German 8.8cm*
20–27 March	British Eighth Army, advancing from east, forces Axis Mareth Line
23 March	US victory at El Guettar against armoured counter-attack
6 April	Battle of Wadi Akarit opens road to Enfidaville to Eighth Army
13 May	Final surrender of Axis forces in Tunisia

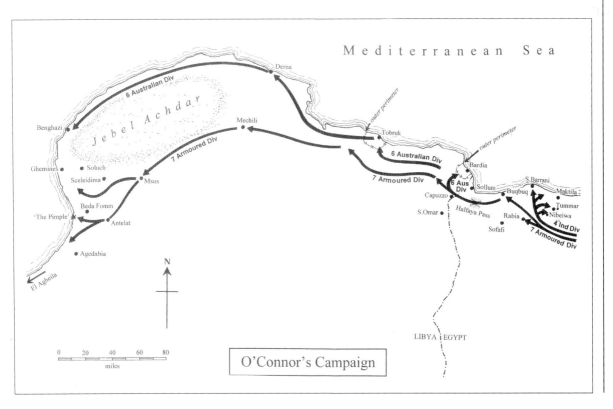

O'Connor's Campaign

THE BRITISH

Starting concepts, 1938–41

During the 1930s the most extreme, persistent and successful advocate of the British Royal Tank Corps (later, Regiment – RTR) had been Gen Patrick ('Percy' or 'Hobo') Hobart, who also happened to be Gen Bernard Montgomery's brother-in-law. His main worry was that in financially difficult times the tanks would be cast to one side by politicans – both inside and outside the army – who wished to spend their budgets elsewhere. In order to make his case Hobart felt obliged to make an unreasonably absolutist claim that the tank could stand almost alone on the modern battlefield. It would not require very much help from the traditional – nay, outdated – arms of horse, foot and gun; it could go forth and conquer on its own, in independent 'fleets' that possessed all the armour, firepower and mobility that they needed. In this he was largely following the influential teachings of J.F.C. ('Boney') Fuller, who had begun to put forward futuristic concepts for tank operations as early as 1917 (but who was unfortunately detached from reality, in more ways than one).

The idea of tanks fighting without all-arms support was based on an assumption that they carried sufficient armour and firepower to win any battle, and could maintain high speeds in all types of terrain. Their main strength would be their ability to achieve surprise by wide outflanking manoeuvres. Meanwhile the other arms, carried in wheeled transport, would be unable to keep up and would, in any case, be vulnerable to the enemy's tanks. This set of beliefs ignored some of the most obvious lessons of 1917, which Fuller more than anyone should have remembered. For example, at Third Ypres the tanks were actually unable to manoeuvre off the roads without bogging, whereas all the other arms could do so. Then at Cambrai – supposedly the tank's finest hour – a single battery of guns was able to halt the attack on the whole of the Flesquières sector. After that it ought to have been axiomatic that the main enemy of the tank was the AT gun; but this was wilfully ignored by the Fuller-Hobart school, who would continue to insist that the best weapon to kill a tank was always another tank.

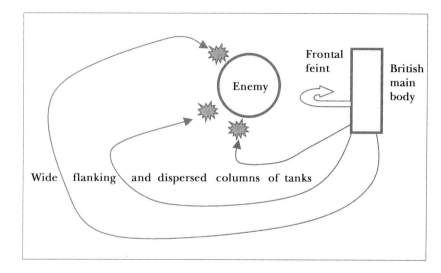

A Fuller-Hobart 'scheme', designed to teach armoured forces to achieve surprise and encirclement by wide outflanking manoeuvres.

Misreading the evidence

These beliefs appeared to be confirmed by the German victories in France in 1940, where it was the Panzers that grabbed all the headlines; but in reality they were under-gunned and thinly armoured, and they always operated in all-arms teams. The power of the Panzer division did not lie in its tanks, as the British newspapers alleged, but in its mobility as an entirely mechanized force of all arms, operating under an umbrella of air superiority. It could act as a fully integrated whole against outdated and much less responsive infantry formations. While German divisions were initially very 'tank heavy', the Panzer generals certainly did not believe in the mistaken 'all-tank' doctrine, and it is remarkable that it persisted for as long as it did in Britain.

One of the main reasons that it did so was the fact that in 1938 Hobart was appointed to command and train the armoured force in Egypt, which he would form into the 7th Armd Div (later to become celebrated for its 'Desert Rat' jerboa symbol). He was dismissed from this post in 1939, but not before sowing the seeds of his pernicious doctrines amongst his pupils. This in itself might not have been disastrous, if only these tactics had failed in the first British offensive by Gen O'Connor during the winter of 1940/41 – such a failure might have caused them to re-think. Unfortunately for British armoured doctrine, however, the Italians gave way all too easily before a series of wide, outflanking surprise attacks, culminating at Beda Fomm in early February, which seemed to fit perfectly into the Fuller-Hobart model. Upon closer inspection it is clear that much of the decisive fighting was actually carried out by all-arms teams that included plenty of infantry and artillery, and the most effective tank turned out to be the heavy Matilda Mk II Infantry (I-) tank, which the purists considered far too slow to keep up with an armoured division. It was therefore untrue that 7th Armd Div had won by applying the Fuller-Hobart doctrines; but that was the myth that was perpetuated.

Egypt, July 1940: a troop of Mk VI Light tanks of 1st RTR halt in line ahead during an exercise with A9 Cruisers (see background). No one is observing the wide dispersion that was holy writ among desert tacticians, but what is written in the manual is not always what happens in practice. Single line ahead was generally only adopted by tanks for road movement. The fast and agile Mk VI – a good hill-climber – had been a useful 'bait' to help lure dashing cavalry officers into accepting mechanization, but in the winter campaign of 1940/41 it proved itself fatally under-gunned and under-armoured. (IWM E 438)

11

Also upon closer inspection, the officers of 7th Armd Div were very conscious that a tank could best deliver its fire if it halted in a 'hull down' position behind a low fold in the ground. (In a 'turret-down' observation position only the commander's hatch on top of the turret was exposed above the line of cover; a 'hull-down' tank exposed just enough of the turret to fire the main gun.) This technique served them well when they held the road block at Beda Fomm on 6–7 February 1941 and beat off successive waves of Italian tanks, totalling over a hundred in all. Elsewhere, however, folds in the ground were often difficult to find in desert terrain. The choice was then between firing at the halt in the open, which gave good accuracy – but also gave the enemy an excellent target; or firing on the move, which decreased accuracy, but also presented a harder target for the enemy. The RTR had a long-standing preference for the latter solution, and trained hard for it, particularly since they had better power-assisted turret rotation than their opponents. They believed that their accuracy was almost as good from a moving tank as from a stationary one, although it is extremely doubtful that this was in fact the case. Fighting on the move fitted well into the whole ethos of mobility that Hobart had tried to instil in his officers; but it also suited German AT gunners very well, when the British attempted it.

The ambiguities of British tactical doctrine were intensified when many of the deeply experienced and efficient personnel of 7th Armd Div, of all ranks, were removed from the front immediately after their victory. They left behind little more than an aura of prestige and a tradition of misleading teachings, which their many inexperienced successors (i.e. the 1st, 2nd, 8th and 10th Armd Divs, as well as several independent armoured brigades) hastened to embrace – they knew no better, and lacked the time to adapt to new circumstances. One thing that confirmed them in their prejudices was the official table of organization of the armoured division as laid down in the late 1930s. This specified that two armoured brigades, each of more than 150 tanks, would be backed up by a 'support group' of just two motorized ('motor') infantry battalions and an artillery brigade. At 'Crusader' in November 1941 there would even be three armoured brigades in 7th Armd Div, making a total of no fewer than 450 tanks. By 1941, in contrast, a Panzer division theoretically had

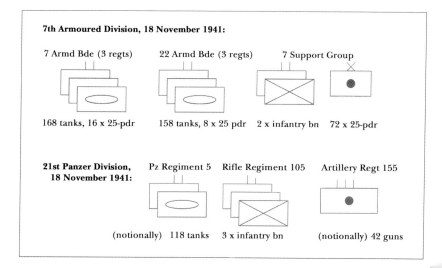

7th Armoured Division, 18 November 1941:

7 Armd Bde (3 regts)   22 Armd Bde (3 regts)   7 Support Group

168 tanks, 16 x 25-pdr   158 tanks, 8 x 25 pdr   2 x infantry bn   72 x 25-pdr

21st Panzer Division, 18 November 1941:   Pz Regiment 5   Rifle Regiment 105   Artillery Regt 155

(notionally) 118 tanks   3 x infantry bn   (notionally) 42 guns

Comparison between basic orders of battle of British and German armoured divisions in the 'Crusader' battles of November 1941.

Derna, 27 December 1941: Sikh infantry of 4th Indian Div practise fire and movement for house-clearing – an art rarely needed in desert warfare. However, once Eighth Army advanced into Cyrenaica it found some coastal terrain that was not unlike the hills and copses of Italy, as well as several fairly substantial towns. (IWM E 7365)

only two tank battalions each of 59 tanks, supported by a brigade of between two and four infantry battalions, as well as an artillery regiment. In other words a British armoured division had as many as 150 tanks per infantry battalion (and 225 at the start of 'Crusader'), whereas the Germans were content to make do with something between 30 and 59 per battalion.

Harbour guards and 'Jock Columns'

All this would have been bad enough in itself, but it was compounded by the attitude that the British armour took towards its own infantry and artillery, including its AT guns. Because the Fuller-Hobart doctrine stipulated that tanks could fight the main battle all on their own, pre-war training had relegated an armoured division's support group to a very auxiliary role. It was supposed to do little more than protect the 'tank harbour' where fuel, ammunition and other supplies would be collected to replenish the weary armoured warriors at the end of their day's combat. There was, in other words, no major desire to involve more than a few detachments of guns and infantry in the 'tank battle' itself. This doctrine was encapsulated in *Army Training Instruction No.3: Handling of an Armoured Division*, which was issued in May 1941. It was repeatedly confirmed in practice, as time and time again we find that the bulk of the British support groups were located elsewhere than the main centres of action. This was a diametrically opposite approach to that of the Germans – and proportionately much less successful. (See Plate D, inset 2.)

The charismatic LtCol J.C. 'Jock' Campbell, VC (of 4th RHA, a part of 7th Armd Div Support Group) appears to have been so bored by this secondary role that as early as September 1940 he had taken it upon himself to organize prowling 'Jock Columns' of all arms *except* tanks, to go out and find opportunities for offensive action against enemy soft-skinned transport. Typically such a column would consist of a battery of 25-pdrs, a company of motor infantry, a troop of armoured cars, a troop of AT guns (2-pdrs), a section of light AA guns (40mm Bofors), plus

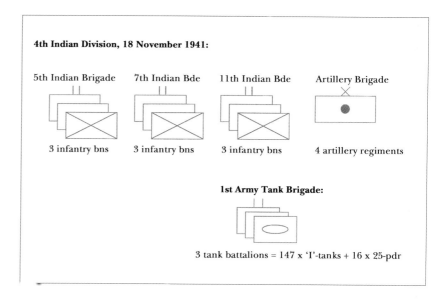

4th Indian Division, 18 November 1941:

5th Indian Brigade	7th Indian Bde	11th Indian Bde	Artillery Brigade
3 infantry bns	3 infantry bns	3 infantry bns	4 artillery regiments

1st Army Tank Brigade:

3 tank battalions = 147 x 'I'-tanks + 16 x 25-pdr

signallers, medics and so forth. Jock Columns would continue in vogue throughout 1941, and even took on a new lease of life at the end of that year, after the main tank forces of both sides had been destroyed in the 'Crusader' fighting. They appeared to represent an aggressively bold initiative to take the battle to the enemy using the maximum of mobility and surprise, while simultaneously giving the support group something useful to do. However, in later days the Jock Columns would be criticized for 'penny-packeting' – a wasteful dispersal of force, particularly of artillery. They were condemned as symbolizing the British habit of fighting with their tanks concentrated in one place, and most of their supporting arms in another. They were also seen as a radical break from the traditional thinking for infantry divisions which, since at least the later stages of the Somme battle in 1916, had been accustomed to fight with all arms well concentrated in one place. This applied especially to their artillery, where an entire brigade of some 72 guns could often expect to fire at a single target, without the type of dispersion and divergent missions that had became customary in 1941 in the desert.

Infantry tanks versus Cruisers

The British problem may in part be attributed to the rigid distinction they made between I-tanks, which were designed to trundle along in close support of infantry, and the Light and Cruiser types, which were supposed to display all the dashing mobility traditionally associated with the cavalry. This distinction was deeply rooted in ancient inter-arm rivalries, but it had been accentuated when most of the proud old British cavalry regiments were mechanized, somewhat abruptly, in 1938. For political reasons they had to be reassured that their basic role remained unchanged, and they tended to be given either armoured cars or the lighter types of tank. However, the RTR, which had traditionally been dismissive and suspicious of the 'horsey' school, had its own traditions which pointed in exactly the same direction.

At Cambrai on 20 November 1917 the tank corps had been frustrated that it did not possess any AFVs capable of fulfilling the break-out role – a role left to the cavalry, who comprehensively failed to carry it out.

It was perhaps Fuller who felt this failure most keenly, and who did most to propagate the idea of the break-out by medium tanks as an alternative. Some progress was made at the battle of Amiens eight months later when, after the heavy tanks had accompanied the infantry onto its first objectives, a more mobile group (including not only cavalry but both armoured cars and Whippet fast tanks) was tasked to break out into 'the green fields beyond'. It did not succeed, but at least it achieved considerably more than the cavalry on its own had managed at Cambrai. During the 1920s and 1930s, therefore, RTR thinking had been focused upon fast – and therefore relatively light – tanks, rather than slow and heavy ones. When it arrived in the desert the RTR was keen to use not only mobility but also its ultimate expression in the head-down charge, or what came to be known – ominously – as 'Balaklavering'.

Infantry doctrine

In the infantry divisions, by contrast, there was a well-understood technique for providing concentrated artillery barrages to help foot-soldiers make short and deliberate steps forward into enemy positions, preferably at night. Ideally I-tanks should be integrated into such plans, in the same auxiliary role that they had successfully fulfilled on the Western Front of 1916–18. In fact, in 1940–43 when an 'army tank brigade' of some 150 tanks was attached to a full infantry division of three brigades, the mixture made for an extremely powerful instrument for limited-range offensives. Indeed, the proportion of armour to the other arms was not very much less than that seen in a German Panzer division, so the chances of success were considerably better than those of the ridiculously over-tanked British armoured divisions.

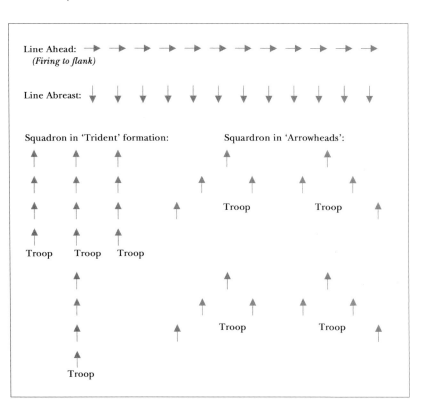

Attack formations for a British tank unit (RTR battalion or armoured cavalry regiment). It seems that formations learned from a manual were never applied with any rigour in real combat. For example, Keith Douglas of the Sherwood Rangers wrote that 'what few words of reminiscence I heard from those who returned from actions in France and the desert suggested that no notice was ever taken of the manoeuvres we had been taught in the field'. The same applied to spacing between vehicles: in theory this should have been more than 100 yards, but in practice it was very variable.

The British Army had been one of the first to introduce near-total mechanization during the late 1930s; but apart from the change in their means of transportation, its infantry divisions remained essentially the same as they had been in 1918. The Bren had replaced the Lewis as the squad light machine gun, and a certain number of armoured carriers were available to carry them – as well as all sorts of other stores – forward into the firing line. The artillery had been updated with the modern 25-pdr gun-howitzer, and there were even a few radios available to every battalion. All this implied a certain increase in the logistic 'tail' needed to service the new vehicles and devices used by the 'teeth' of the front line troops. Otherwise, however, the infantry division remained almost exactly as it had been in the final phases of the Great War. Its men lived in slit trenches, from which they emerged to fight mainly at night. When they did, they were often extremely effective, especially when well supported by artillery and I-tanks. But in desert conditions their motor transport often had to be pulled back well out of sight of the enemy, thus robbing them of mobility. This circumstance led immediately to the infantry bleating for tank support, which was rarely forthcoming but produced many recriminations. Relations between British infantry and armour were rarely harmonious, apart from the special case of the 'army tank brigades' of I-tanks dedicated to support particular infantry formations.

THE ITALIANS

The first opponent the British had to face were the Italians, who wanted to capture Egypt but did not have their first-line troops available to do the job. In particular they were short of motor transport, which meant that their infantry was almost completely immobile and often short of supplies. They were also badly deficient in armour: alongside 14 infantry divisions there was only one Italian armoured brigade in Libya in January 1941, and its vehicles were of poor quality. It soon became clear that the Italian generals were much better warriors than their junior officers, NCOs and other ranks. They knew perfectly well how to lay out fortified camps with good minefields and artillery support, and in Bardia and Tobruk with concrete pillboxes and anti-tank ditches too. However, their infantry – and especially their supposedly élite 'Blackshirt' Fascist militia – were badly trained and equipped. They could not make anything like the best use of the defensive works provided for them, and they were easily cut off by British mobile columns appearing from the rear. In winter 1940/41 their defences crumbled completely, as soon as a well-organized night attack was launched by British Empire infantry and artillery supported by Matilda I-tanks. If held by troops of better quality, the same fortifications could have held out much better, as was proved by the staunch resistance of the mainly Australian garrison of Tobruk during the eight-month siege that began in April 1941.

The Italian army was chronically short not just of training, transport, equipment and supplies but also of experienced company officers and NCOs. As a result its tactics were generally rigid and hidebound; since there were too few natural leaders at platoon and company level, to breathe flexibility and responsiveness into the system, they could not

respond rapidly if something went wrong – as it almost invariably did. In these circumstances attacks were almost always foredoomed to be predictably frontal and sacrificial, while defences would be static and linear, without the benefit of counter-attacks or active concepts of defence. All this meant that Graziani's army fought badly, suffered too much, and surrendered in droves (over nine divisions were destroyed). It created an indelible stereotype of military inefficiency and a reliable source of mirth to the British population, at a time when such consolations for their own heavy losses and grinding hardships were in short supply.

What the stereotype concealed was the renaissance in Italian military competence that followed almost immediately after the defeat at Beda Fomm in February 1941. Reforms of the system were being pushed through in Italy, not least of which was the suppression of the political (and mainly non-military) Blackshirt divisions in favour of much more combat-effective regiments, as corps troops. Meanwhile in Libya five infantry divisions remained standing, and were soon reinforced, reconstituted and up-gunned. Under Rommel's inspired leadership they would soon move back onto the offensive. Admittedly, they still lacked much of the motor transport they needed; but once they had arrived outside Tobruk they could be used in the static role to which they were accustomed. Manning the lines of investment around the fortress, they gradually accumulated useful combat experience with every month that passed. Most significant of all, perhaps, was the arrival of the 'Ariete' armoured, 'Trento' and then 'Trieste' motorized divisions, making the first serious commitment of Italian mechanized forces to this theatre. These were veteran formations, including units originally blooded in combat during the Spanish Civil War under the command of Gen Bastico, who now came to Libya himself.

An Italian infantry platoon make a practice attack, 1942. They are attempting to use fire and movement, but really they are in Great War-style lines, and bunched criminally closely together given the absolute absence of any cover. Despite the notoriously poor reliability of the 6.5mm M1930 Breda light machine gun, the presence of four of them among the 20-odd men visible here is still an impressively high scale of issue. The central figure with a slung carbine is the officer. (Private collection)

Italians of the 'Pavia' infantry division inspecting (or servicing?) a British A9 Cruiser tank captured from 1st RTR in September 1940. This intriguing photo was taken in July 1942, and the tank has clearly been pressed into Italian service, perhaps for infantry support within this division – after unguessable adventures during the intervening two years of fast-moving campaigning. (Private collection)

Improvement in 1941/42

'Ariete' and 'Trieste' would together become XX Mobile Corps, and would cast Italian operations in a new and much more impressive mould. The wake-up call for the British came at Bir el Gubi on 19 November 1941, when Brig Scott-Cockburn's 22nd Armd Bde blundered into their midst without reconnaissance and with just eight field guns in support. The Italians fought back tenaciously, and their 132nd Tank Regt launched a telling counter-attack. Within the space of less than four hours the British brigade had been reduced to about half of its tank strength, and according to one report had only ten 'runners' left by dusk. This battle should have delivered a body-blow to the popular stereotype of the Italian soldier, formed by the earlier photographs of acres of cheerfully complacent prisoners of war strolling into captivity; but it was not really recognized as such at the time, and it has remained largely under-reported in the British literature right up to the present day.

Even Mussolini's political troops were fighting well by this time, as the 'Giovani Fascisti' mechanized reconnaissance group demonstrated on 4 December, again at Bir el Gubi, when it beat off several attacks by 11th Indian Brigade. The Italians were again in a static defensive role; but on this occasion they did stick to their guns, and achieved effective all-arms co-ordination between infantry, field artillery, AT guns and light tanks.

At the battle of Gazala in May–June 1942 the Italians again had an important role to play in Rommel's plans, both as a screen of infantry to pin British Empire forces in the northern section of the line, and with XX Corps forming part of his mobile spearhead to swing around the southern flank. The latter saw particularly hard fighting, and was able to keep up all the way through to Alamein in July, following close behind the DAK vanguard. During this period the Italians were reinforced by the 'Littorio' armoured and 'Folgore' parachute divisions, both of which fought well until they were finally swept away in the general defeat of early November. Indeed, all the Italian troops in the Alamein line discharged their duties faithfully, and were unable to make a fighting retreat only because their German allies stole all their motor transport and fuel.

Summer 1941: the crew of a *Deutsches Afrika Korps* PzKw III Ausf G relax, read their mail and conduct personal grooming; the tank guns are covered to protect the bore from the damaging abrasion of airborne grit. In the desert the PzKw III was the German equivalent of what the British called a 'Cruiser' tank – in other words, its main task was to take on British armour and fight what was conventionally (but often misleadingly) called a 'tank battle'. This unit seems to be halted in sand-and-gravel desert with plentiful scrub; despite its low height this made excellent disruptive camouflage for dug-in AT guns. (Private collection)

As Tunisia fell under threat from both east and west during the winter of 1942/43 both of the Axis powers hastened to send in reinforcements. Again the Italians fought well, despite the scarcity and obsolescence of their weaponry. They were particularly boosted by the arrival of Gen Messe, who had enjoyed an excellent combat record on the Russian Front, and was arguably the one man who might have averted Axis defeat at Stalingrad if only he had been maintained in his command there. Nevertheless, by the time he arrived in Tunisia the whole strategic position had been fatally compromised by two years' under-resourcing. A particular cause of this was Mussolini's sending of an unnecessarily large army of ten divisions to Russia, accompanied by no fewer than 22,000 trucks. Even a quarter of those resources might have saved the day in Africa if only they had been available there in 1942.

THE GERMANS

In stark contrast to both the British and Italians, the Germans had intensively studied large-scale mobile operations since at least 1866, and indeed since the staffwork of Scharnhorst, Gneisenau and Clausewitz in Napoleonic times. The Germans also came to Libya with extensive recent experience of mechanized warfare, its seeds sown back in 1936 when an armoured instruction and observation mission had been sent to Spain. In the 1940 French campaign the British had managed to throw little more than one armoured brigade into the battle, while the Germans had fielded ten whole Panzer divisions. It was not even true that they had derived much intellectual stimulation from British post-1918 theorists of mobile warfare. Dubious characters such as Fuller or B.H. Liddell Hart later variously claimed that they had; and some German generals, not least Heinz Guderian, were persuaded to agree, at a time when they were vulnerable in captivity. However, the record seems to be clear that they never really meant it.[3]

---

[3] These issues are discussed in J. Mearsheimer, *Liddell Hart and the Weight of History*, Cornell (Ithaca, 1988)

German 10.5cm lfH 18 field gun, the mainstay of Rommel's artillery. Unlike his British opponents in 1941, he believed in starting any action by the maximum use of firepower, especially HE from artillery and PzKw IV tanks. His experiences in France in May 1940 led him to write: 'I have found again and again that in encounter actions, the day goes to the side that is the first to plaster its opponent with fire.' (Private collection)

The reality is that German staff officers before 1941 had developed their own ideas about mechanized warfare, based upon the long historical traditions of their military doctrine, which included the need to make an objective analysis of each new machine or weapon as it became available. This was in sharp contrast to those British theorists who believed, in a mystical sort of way, that the tank had suddenly overthrown all past ideas about warfare, and would by definition always be victorious without reference to any other factor. We might say that whereas the British were 'creationists' in this area, the Germans were firmly wedded to 'evolution'. It also helped them that in the 1930s Hitler lent his personal authority to the creation of a unified Panzer arm which would not, as in Britain, be a collection of many different cap badges all struggling, instinctively, to retain their historic identities. Whether or not they belonged to newly raised units, all members of a Panzer division were encouraged to think of themselves first and foremost as members of a new and élite formation, working together in a pragmatic way, and even the titles of the non-tank units were often prefixed by the magic word *Panzer*.

Tactical principles

Some of the tactical principles that the Germans embraced, but which the British usually did not, were as follows:

(a) A mechanized striking force should always operate with all arms in a close grouping. Wide dispersion was not an ideal to be encouraged, especially at times when the Luftwaffe enjoyed a superiority over the RAF.

(b) In an all-arms grouping, the speed of the whole was necessarily that of the slowest vehicle. Thus the tanks were forbidden from racing off over the horizon and leaving everyone else behind; nor should they venture into ground that was impassable to all the other vehicles, except very locally. In any case, high speed was not a particularly desirable quality in a tank, although mechanical reliability was definitely a high priority for all vehicles.

(c) If vehicles broke down, it was essential to recover them and get them repaired without delay. Mechanical repairs were an essential element in mobility, especially when (as was usually the case in the desert war) the German tanks were rather heavily outnumbered by Allied tanks. Equally there was a great dividend to be won by holding the battlefield at the end of a day's fighting, so that damaged vehicles could be recovered.

(d) Repairing vehicles in darkness is ridiculously difficult unless you use floodlights. This may well give away your position to the enemy; but at least you will have more vehicles running in the morning, when the enemy is ready to attack you.

(e) The cohesion of an all-arms force relies heavily upon good radio communication. No resources spent to that end will ever be wasted (and by the same token, it is noticeable that all the way up to the first battle of Alamein, the DAK enjoyed a marked superiority over Eighth Army in intercepting and interpreting enemy transmissions).

(f) Perhaps most important of all – firepower was the key to any battle, as Rommel had already clearly laid down in the 1940 campaign in France. Before you did anything else, you had to flail the enemy positions, and especially his AT weapons, with a heavy bombardment of HE shells. Only after that could you decide whether or not he had been weakened enough for you to launch an assault. The HE should be fired by PzKw IV tanks at a range of around 2,000 metres, and by field artillery from a little further back.

(g) At every stage there must be a high level of reconnaissance: first to identify enemy strength and dispositions, and later to determine exactly how well he has been suppressed by firepower. The initial attack by firepower would be converted into a full-blooded advance to close range only if the commander was convinced that the defending AT guns had been suppressed. If this did not happen, the Germans would usually pull back and call off the whole operation. Only on a very few exceptional occasions would higher operational orders overrule the purely tactical decisions of the commander on the spot.

Rommel in his Horch staff car, beside an Italian M13/40 tank. The 'Desert Fox' was notorious for his insatiable desire to be present at the _Schwerpunkt_ (key point, or point of maximum effort) of any battle, to improve his understanding of what was going on and thereby speed up his command reactions. By contrast, his British counterparts commanding Eighth Army almost always stayed back, working through a long chain of command (via regiment, brigade, division and corps), every link of which added time to the transmission of reports and then the issue of orders. It could often take 24 hours for the British to react to a new situation, and for Operation 'Aberdeen' at Gazala in early June 1942 it would take the best part of a week. (Tank Museum 3182/B2)

(h) It is not very clear whether or not this stress on reconnaissance included the idea of infantry patrolling on foot, which certainly played an important part in traditional British – and even more so, Australian – doctrine. To the present author it seems that it did not, and that the German concept of reconnaissance was all about motor vehicles.

Beyond these basic and fundamental principles, the Germans also exhibited a number of lesser tactical 'tricks'. An important one was to use AT guns in an offensive as well as a purely defensive role, so that wherever there was a tank, there would also be a towed AT gun ready to come into action at a moment's notice. This often caught the British by surprise; in effect, it doubled the AT firepower of any given column of vehicles – and often without the low-slung towed guns being visible from a distance, since they would be concealed in the huge plumes of dust raised by the tanks and by the trucks that were towing them. Another tactical habit was to attack out of a low sun in order to blind the enemy gunners, which against Eighth Army normally meant driving eastwards towards the end of the day.

Yet another was a habit of leading from the front, especially by Rommel himself. He was liable to turn up wherever the fighting was hottest, to direct the local battle in person. This often had a beneficial effect on the outcome within his own field of vision; but equally it drove his staff to distraction, since it meant he was often absent from his central HQ when important operational decisions had to be taken. He has sometimes been criticized for being the best battalion commander in the army, but perhaps not the finest staff officer.

THE BALANCE OF HARDWARE

As for the tanks themselves, the **British** had too few funds available during the inter-war period for the proper development of AFVs. There always seemed to be awkward industrial reasons why no tank could be built which combined good speed with good armour. This in turn played neatly into the existing doctrinal mindset by which any given

Knocked-out British 2-pdr (40mm) AT gun, shot square through the gunshield during the post-'Crusader' fighting in December 1941. The damage appears to have been done by a 5cm AP shell, which might have been fired by either a towed AT gun or a PzKw III. The 2-pdr should have been replaced by the much more powerful 6-pdr (57mm) during 1941, but the production programme was set back a year by the losses incurred in France in 1940. The first 6-pdr AT batteries would arrive only for the battle of Gazala in May 1942. ` (IWM E 7060)

Comparison of tank crews fuels and radios

For maximum efficiency a tank should normally have a 4- or 5-man crew. It was logistically more convenient if it ran on petrol/gasoline rather than either diesel (which was less flammable if the tank was hit) or high-octane 'avgas' – aviation gasoline (which was more flammable). Note that this list omits specialist command, close support etc variants.

Tank	Crew	Fuel	Radios
German:			
PzKw I	2	petrol	Command tanks, 2 transceivers
PzKw II	3	petrol	Platoon leaders, initially 1 transceiver, others receiver only; later, all had transceivers
PzKw III	5	petrol	as above
PzKw IV	5	petrol	as above
Italian:			
L3/CV3	2	petrol	none
M11/39	3	petrol	none
M13/ & 14/40	4	diesel	none
British:			
A12/ Matilda II	4	diesel	transceiver
Valentine	3*	diesel	transceiver
Light Mk VI	3	petrol	transceiver
A9/ Cruiser Mk I	6	petrol	transceiver
A10/ Cruiser Mk II	4 (5 in IIA)	petrol	transceiver
A13/ Cruiser Mk IV, Mk IVA, & A15/ Mk VI Crusader	4**	petrol	transceiver
US:			
M3 Stuart/ Honey	4	avgas	transceiver
M3 Grant	6	avgas	transceiver
M4 Sherman	5	avgas	transceiver

* The original cramped turret was later enlarged to accommodate a fourth crewman
** Early Crusaders had a cramped auxiliary MG turret, so needed a 5-man crew if this was manned; it was found excessive in action, and discontinued. In late 1942 the Mk III, with 6-pdr gun, accommodated only 3 crew.

vehicle should have either one or the other quality, but not both at once. The Desert Rats did not complain, until it was too late, that they had to choose between fast but lightly armoured Cruisers and slow but heavy I-tanks. Only the American M4 Sherman (developed from the M3 Lee and Grant) would eventually exhibit a truly satisfactory balance between speed and armour, but it would become available only in late 1942, when it can be argued that it was already approaching obsolescence. (Shamefully, the ideal British-built 'capital' or 'main battle' tank, in the shape of the excellent A41 Centurion, would take the field only in the very last days of the war, when it was far too late.)

In the field of tank armament the British suffered from two major limitations. The first was that their plans to replace their 2-pdr (40mm) AT gun by a 6-pdr (57mm) were set back by a year when much of the existing inventory of 2-pdrs were lost in the Dunkirk campaign. For industrial reasons it was felt preferable to fill the gaps with large numbers of the old design, rather than with the much smaller numbers of the new one that could be made available in the same time. By 1941 the 2-pdr was far from being the best AT gun in the world, but it was, nevertheless, the best one mounted on any tank in North Africa: it had greater penetration against Axis tanks than the latter had penetration against British ones. In a purely tank-vs-tank contest the British might have cause for complaint that their armour was thinner than their enemies', but they could scarcely claim that their guns were less powerful.

Italian M13/40 tanks, probably of 133rd Regt of the 'Littorio' Div, advancing in line abreast near Mechili, Cyrenaica, in March 1942. According to British tactical theory they are rather closely bunched, but they are conforming more with German tactical theory (and with frequent British practice). The M13/40 was obsolete by this date, but it was the best the Italians had. Wartime jokes notwithstanding, its crews often fought with great courage and determination. (Private collection)

The 6-pdr AT gun would not come into British service until the spring of 1942, and its successor, the mighty 17-pdr (76.2mm), only as late as March 1943; and both of these were towed guns. Tank-mounted versions would have to wait much longer; only 100 Crusader Mk III tanks mounted the 6-pdr at Second Alamein in October 1942, followed by some 6-pdr Churchill Mk IIIs in Tunisia in January 1943. Almost all other British-built tanks before the end of 1942 were equipped with 2-pdrs – apart from a very few which had close support howitzers, and the very lightest types that carried nothing heavier than machine guns. The American M3 Stuarts (which the British called 'Honeys') had a 37mm gun roughly comparable to the 2-pdr; and it was only the arrival of the American M3 Grant in the spring of 1942, and that of the M4 Sherman later in the year, that would bring a heavier (75 mm) gun. This was doubly welcome because, unlike the 2-pdr (but in common with the 6-pdr), it was capable of firing HE as well as AP shells.

The second limitation was that the turret rings of all the British-designed tanks at that time had a relatively small diameter, which meant that there was little scope to build the larger turrets that would be needed to mount heavier guns. Thus, when the 6-pdr was mounted on a Crusader Mk III it took up so much space that the crew had to be reduced by one man, making for an incomplete team and consequent difficulties in 'fighting' the tank smoothly. By contrast, the German PzKw III and IV had rather bigger turret rings, so they could be up-gunned more easily as better weapons successively became available. By the second half of 1942 a few of these tanks in North Africa were already being equipped with considerably better AT guns than anything available on Allied tanks, in the shape of long 5cm and 7.5cm pieces respectively. Finally, in Tunisia a handful of PzKw VI Tiger tanks took the field with a version of the 8.8cm gun that had already taken a heavy toll of Allied tanks as a towed dual-purpose (AA and AT) gun. It would be another 18 months before the Allies could fit a comparable weapon into any of their own tanks.

The armour/ AT gun race

Max. tank armour thickness	AT gun penetration
(German was variable, due to factory & local addition of extra plates, some spaced)	(against homogenous armour, at 1,000 yards, at 30° angle of strike)
Allied tanks:	*Axis guns:*
A15 Crusader – 49mm	3.7cm – 22mm
M3 Stuart – 44mm	Italian 47mm – 29mm
Matilda Mk II – 78mm	5cm short – 47mm
Mk III Valentine – 65mm	5cm long – 55mm
A22 Churchill – 102mm	7.5cm short – 41mm
M3 Grant – 57mm	7.5cm long – 72mm
M4 Sherman – 91mm	8.8cm – 101mm
Axis tanks:	*Allied guns:*
PzKw III – 40mm	2-pdr (40mm) – 40mm
Italian M13/40 – 40mm	37mm – 42mm
PzKw III J – 50mm	25-pdr (88mm) AP – 54mm
PzKw IV – 30mm	6-pdr (57mm) 80mm
PzKw IV F – 50mm	75mm – 62mm
PzKw VI Tiger – 110mm	17-pdr (76.2mm) – 118mm

On the Axis side, the **Italian** tanks were obsolescent from the first and were never seriously up-graded. Their L3/35 was essentially equivalent to the British Bren carrier, and was armed only with machine guns. The M11 mounted its 37mm gun only in the hull, while any hit on its glacis plate was likely to start a major fire in the transmission fluid. The more modern M13 tank, with a 47mm gun, was considered just about good enough for the British to run a battalion (6th RTR) of captured examples in the spring of 1941; but they never really performed well, being notoriously underpowered and unreliable. Their armour was also slightly thinner than that of the Crusader and Stuart.

The **Germans** had actually started the war with even lighter tanks than the British. Neither the PzKw I or II was a serious fighting vehicle for

The widely (and justifiably) feared 8.8cm Flak 36 in the ground role. Its high muzzle velocity and excellent optical sights gave it an effective range of over 2,000 yards, while the heavy weight of its shell made a solid hit fatal to any known AFV. Some British tank crews who experienced near-misses reported actually seeing a track of flying dust racing towards them in the moving shock wave beneath the flying shell, like the track of a torpedo at sea. (Private collection)

Turret of a PzKw IV with the short 7.5cm gun, showing a binocular rangefinder in use. One of the Germans' tactical advantages lay in their superior optical instruments, which helped them to deliver accurate fire at long ranges; typically the PzKw IV would fire HE from around 2,000 yards. The British eventually realized that they were being 'out-telescoped', which only reinforced their feelings of inferiority when faced by DAK Panzers. However, in desert conditions even the best optics were often frustrated by the dust that vehicles threw up, or by the distortions created by heat hazes; the hottest part of the day, in mid afternoon, was often a very difficult time to fight a battle. Note the memorial plaque to a dead crewman, painted over the vision slot beside the bow MG-gunner's position. (Tank Museum 7417/A4)

anything more than reconnaissance, and they should be seen as something between a heavy armoured car and a Bren carrier. Although many were landed in Tripoli at the start of the German intervention, they wasted away quite quickly by a Darwinian process whereby only the fittest survived. For the German tank park the fittest meant the PzKw III, which in 1941 mounted a short 5cm AT gun, and the robust PzKw IV, which had a short 7.5cm low-velocity cannon for firing HE. In fact the PzKw IV – at first issued to only one company per battalion, but later representing almost half the German tanks in theatre – would normally fire little else. Despite widespread British belief to the contrary, its AT capability was unspectacular. This vehicle had originally been designed as an I-tank, to suppress enemy guns and infantry from long range rather than to engage tanks directly; for most of the desert war it was only the PzKw III, with its short 5cm gun, that was optimized to kill tanks. (Only a handful of the more formidable PzKw IV F2, with a long, high-velocity 7.5cm tank-killing gun, reached the desert at the end of August 1942.) The PzKw III was less heavily armoured than the IV, and in many ways evenly matched with the most modern British Cruisers; yet it could still fire HE, while the British had to go through the cumbersome process of appealing to their field artillery if they wanted it.

It was also an advantage to the Germans that their tanks' armour-piercing shot was not simply a solid bolt of metal, such as that fired by the British 2-pdr, but contained a small explosive charge designed to detonate after penetration had been achieved. This created a fire hazard which, if the round landed near stowed ammunition or petrol lines, could lead to something much more catastrophic than just the hole made by a solid shot. Overall it was noticeable in the desert that British tanks tended to catch fire more often than German when they were hit.

Of course, the efficiency of any tank rests upon much more than its balance between armour, speed and firepower. In particular it also needs good mechanical reliability and excellent radios, both of which left much to be desired in British and especially Italian tanks. There were often good reasons for this, not least the fact that the whole supporting bureaucracy for recovery, maintenance and repairs had to be reinvented almost from scratch for mobile warfare in desert conditions. If it did nothing else, the desert war provoked many remarkable advances in all these fields, in the British case leading to the creation of the Royal Electrical & Mechanical Engineers (REME). Nevertheless, it was an activity in which the Germans often enjoyed an important advantage, not least because they seemed to be rather better at 'holding the field of slaughter' at the end of any given day of battle, and were therefore better able to recover their damaged tanks. Equally, the Germans were famous for their excellent optical instruments, especially range-finders, which led British commentators to conclude that they were being 'out-telescoped'.

Anti-tank guns

It is important to note that in any battle a significant proportion of the AT fire suffered by British tanks did not come from other tanks at all, as perhaps British tacticians liked to assume, but from towed (ground-mounted) AT guns. The German 5cm gun was particularly potent, and their famous 8.8cm Flak gun even more so, although it was available in far smaller numbers. British tank crews often imagined that they were being hit by tank fire when in fact they were being hit by something much more serious; the literature is crammed with examples of this misconception.[4] This led them to make a false comparison between the supposed power of the Axis tank guns and the perceived weakness of their own – which in turn reinforced the British belief that they did not particularly need to fire HE shells at the enemy. High explosive was not a good weapon against tanks, but was ideal against AT guns. Since the British doctrinal mindset was pre-occupied with tanks fighting other tanks, it simply did not take account of the need to shell AT guns with HE – in diametrical opposition to the German perception of what was needed.

The British believed that they themselves possessed an adequate anti-tank defence, although it was split into five distinct and different elements. The first was the infantry platoon's 0.55in Boys AT rifle, which could be useful against very light armour, or sometimes against the flank or rear of heavier tanks, but for nothing much else. The next were the 2-pdr guns fitted on tanks, and the ballistically identical 2-pdr towed guns on ground mountings or portee vehicle mounts. While these guns were recognized as being the best in their category, by 1942 that whole category had become practically obsolete. The fourth prop of British AT defences was provided by the Bofors 40mm quick-firing AA gun, which in practice did some good service with AP shells, but was not often available at the key time or place. Finally and most importantly, there was the incomparable 25-pdr gun-howitzer. This was in fact almost precisely an 8.8cm weapon, although its muzzle velocity was considerably lower than that of the 8.8cm Flak. There were many occasions on which 25-pdrs in the AT role did succeed in beating off the Panzers. A major disadvantage, of course, was that as long as they were firing AP ammunition they could not be firing HE; their dual role thus served to reduce the availability of HE to the British in a 'tank battle' still further.

A sixth potential British AT weapon was the 3.7in (92mm) AA gun, which was ballistically better than the German 8.8cm Flak. The question has often been asked why it was not widely used in the same way, to which the answers are many and complicated. There were problems with sights – of which three different types were tried before an effective AT sight was developed – and with the production of AP ammunition. It took about ten minutes to remove the wheels and unfold the static firing

---

4 See, for example, J.A.I. Agar-Hamilton & L.C.F. Turner, *The Sidi Rezeg Battles*, Oxford UP (Cape Town, 1957), p.39

The A22/ Churchill Mk I close support I-tank, with a 2-pdr AT gun in the turret and a 3in howitzer in the hull front; as in the M3 Grant, this excessively low mounting prevented tanks from firing their main armament from hull-down positions. At government insistence the A22 was rushed into production so prematurely that its many defects led the manufacturers, Vauxhall Motors, to issue a written apology and disclaimer with each tank delivered. Nevertheless, in later Marks – with a conventional main gun mounting in the turret – it would become reliable and popular. At Longstop Hill in Tunisia, on 26 April 1943, Mk IIIs with 6-pdr guns surprised and defeated the enemy by their unexpected ability to scale steeper gradients than any other known tank; the corps commander called the Churchills his 'mountain goats'. (Tank Museum collection; author's photo)

platform, and the sheer height of the beast, which did not have a gunshield, made it a more vulnerable target than its German equivalent (although firing both guns kicked up a 100-foot dust cloud). There were also 'political' pressures for it to be kept nearer to the Army, Navy and RAF rear base areas than to the front line where it might encounter Panzers. All of these difficulties had been solved in theory by the summer of 1942 (notably by the energetic efforts of Brig Percy Calvert, commander of the 4th Heavy Anti-Aircraft Bde), but with very few exceptions the 3.7in was still not used against tanks.

It is hard to avoid the conclusion that this was ultimately because British doctrine saw all AT guns as defensive and static weapons, and therefore not really appropriate to take part in a mobile tank battle. If friendly tanks were defeated and forced to fall back upon their AT guns, then all well and good; but pushing the guns forward to accompany an armoured thrust somehow went against the grain. The Germans, by contrast, regarded the deployment of AT guns – including even the heaviest – as an integral part of all tank movements, in the advance no less than the retreat.

FROM 'BREVITY' AND 'BATTLEAXE' TO 'CRUSADER'

May–December 1941

In late April 1941 the Germans took over the lead from the Italians, and surprised the British by the speed of their advance into Cyrenaica. In the region of Benghazi they all but destroyed the 2nd Armd Div – although, since it was newly arrived, badly equipped and numerically weak its disappearance was perhaps less shocking to British tacticians than it might otherwise have been. They could soon draw reassurance from the solidity of the defence at Tobruk, and from the expiry of the enemy offensive on the Egyptian frontier. The British art of defence was not, it seemed, an entirely hopeless case. When it came to the art of attack, by contrast, it was soon apparent that the methods that had worked well against Graziani's Italians were no longer dependable against Rommel's Afrika Korps. Apart from anything else, the enemy could no longer be relied upon to stand immobile in one place while the British armour pirouetted around him.

Two attacks were attempted from the Egyptian frontier towards Halfaya, Sollum and Capuzzo, but both failed. The first was Operation 'Brevity' on 15–16 May, although it was perhaps mounted on too small a scale to make a fair test, with just two armoured battalions and but 53 tanks. The British retired almost as soon as their over–dispersed forces were threatened by an advancing Panzer regiment – which itself, in the event, believed it was badly outnumbered, and managed to run out of fuel at the critical moment. In tactical terms this operation underlined the weakness of British signals and inter-arm co-operation when their forces became dispersed – most notably when the Cruiser tanks had dashed off into the west, leaving the infantry far behind. When deserted by their tanks in this way the infantry became inordinately worried for their own safety; the spectre of the 'ten-foot-high Panzer' (which had haunted the battlefields of France and Greece) took a hold on their imagination that would not be shaken off for well over a year.

The second attack was Operation 'Battleaxe' on 15–17 June; with four tank battalions totalling 190 tanks, this was more than three times the size of 'Brevity'. Unfortunately, however, the intervening month had given Rommel a corresponding opportunity to strengthen his own preparations, not least by scattering a 15-mile-deep web of self-sufficient strongpoints around the frontier area. The single most memorable tactical event of the battle came when C Sqn, 4th RTR lost all 12 of its tanks attacking the Halfaya Pass, at what had previously been considered the impossibly long range of 1,500 yards. This was doubly shocking since the destroyed tanks were Matildas, a model that had previously been regarded, by both sides, as particularly well armoured and difficult to knock out. British commentators speculated for many weeks thereafter about just what sort of secret weapon could possibly have done the damage, and there were some who believed it must have been at least a 6in (155mm) high-velocity gun. The killer was in fact a battery of four German 8.8cm (3.5in) AA guns, a weapon which was already known to be deadly against tanks. It is remarkable that it took British tacticians so long to work out that the mysterious 'Halfaya gun' was indeed none other than the familiar 'Eighty-eight'.

Elsewhere during 'Battleaxe' many of the problems that had been seen during 'Brevity' reappeared – most notably, excessive dispersion and inadequate radio power for controlling a fluid, ever-changing situation. On this occasion, however, there was a great deal more combat than had been seen in May, and on Hafid Ridge the British would encounter a phenomenon that would become almost typical in subsequent battles. This was the allure of an enemy position that appeared to be only lightly defended, or occupied only by vulnerable soft-skinned vehicles. The temptation would be strong for British armour to charge in piecemeal and without careful preparation, leading to disastrous results when the enemy's 'vulnerable' trucks turned out to be accompanied by towed guns, some of which proved to be very dangerous indeed to attacking tanks. On Hafid Ridge this problem was made worse by the complexities of the terrain, which turned out to consist of three successive ridges rather than just one; the Axis forces lurking behind the second and third caused all sorts of unexpected difficulties to the British armour that had successfully cleared the first. This battle therefore stands as a classic early example of all those difficulties of reconnaissance, navigation and terrain analysis that proved such pitfalls for tacticians throughout the whole desert war.

Then again, 'Battleaxe' also saw some passages of 'pure' tank-vs-tank combat such as had been so widely discussed before the war. For example, the after-action reports of 6th RTR show that the battalion performed a long series of recognizably 'naval' manoeuvres on 15–16 June, with squadrons repeatedly manoeuvring in line ahead, delivering 'a good broadside shoot at speed' (i.e. to a flank, firing on the move); this fitted exactly into the old naval ideal of 'crossing the enemy's T'.[5]

It seems that this battalion had already lost about 17 of its 52 Crusader tanks as a result of mechanical breakdowns on their journey from the Alexandria docks, where they had been unloaded from the 'Tiger' convoy. Once in battle, 6th RTR then lost 15 tanks on 15 June, and 12 more on the 16th, making a total of 41. Of this total, 14 were recovered as 'crocks', some of which were certainly damaged by mechanical defects rather than by enemy fire. Thus, although the battalion ceased to be an effective fighting force after just two days in action, the loss of only about half of its initial 52 tanks can be attributed to the enemy. We can even suggest that it was a relatively bloodless battle, with only nine members of the battalion believed killed (or at least, it was bloodless enough for survivors to regard 'tank fighting' as a less than suicidal activity). In fact, 6th RTR experienced only one moment of really serious casualties, when it charged over Hafid Ridge at about 1745hrs on 15 June, losing three tanks from A Sqn and 10 from B, of which four were later recovered. For the rest of the battle the tank losses came only in ones and twos, as a steady trickle of background attrition but nothing especially dramatic. Indeed, desert warfare as a whole could often seem to be an indecisive and even inconsequential process, in which large numbers of gas-guzzling vehicles, both armoured and unarmoured, growled around each other raising billowing clouds of dust but rarely even exchanging shots. By the end of each day everyone would be completely exhausted;

Derna, 5 January 1941: an Australian examines an Italian AT mine. At this stage of the campaign minefields were still relatively small and represented only a minor nuisance. However, by 1942 anti-tank and anti-personnel mines would be laid literally in millions, becoming a near-dominant factor that shaped every battlefield, and a major limitation on the mobility of armoured forces. They would be used to great effect by the British at Gazala and First Alamein, and by the Axis at Second Alamein. The main threat of AT mines lay in their ability to blow the tracks off any tank, regardless of the quality of its hull armour; they could, of course, also be deadly to men in lighter vehicles or caught while accompanying the armour on foot. This mine seems to be filled with 3.2kg of TNT – eight 200g blocks at each end, linked by detcord (instantaneous fuse) from the inwards-pointing detonator wells in each of the 'blank-topped' blocks, through an ignition mechanism initiated by sufficient pressure on the two strong coil springs; two 'windows' give access for arming and disarming. (IWM E 1890)

[5] The diagrams are reproduced in Jentz, pp.169, 176

yet they would still have to face many more laborious hours of leaguering, replenishing and re-fitting before they could snatch a few short hours of sleep. In these circumstances the outcome often looked more like a 'victory on points', won by whichever side could stay active in the field for longest, rather than the sort of knockout blow which fuelled the dreams of armchair strategists.

One of the main tactical lessons of 'Battleaxe' was that British tanks had little chance of knocking out German tanks at ranges of much more than 600–800 yards, whereas British tanks were being knocked out at much longer ranges than that. British tank crews were therefore reinforced in their desire to charge in to close range where they could do some damage. That

Late April 1941: hand signals signifying 'Advance' from an A13 Cruiser Mk II tank of 5th RTR. Note the sun-compass mounted close to the nearer tank commander's right elbow – see photo on page 3. (IWM E 2639)

was reasonable enough, although a number of key points were missed by British tacticians. In the first place they had little idea about either the ballistic qualities or the active forward employment of German AT guns, as the strange head-scratching over the 'Halfaya gun' reveals. Secondly, they failed to understand that German tacticians believed their own tanks' guns and armour to be scarcely better than the British, and thus that it was a priority to protect them by manoeuvring behind AT screens. Whenever possible, German tanks were to act cautiously and avoid charging in to close range. Meanwhile every effort was devoted to improving their tanks' armour, both by adding special face-hardened plates and by hanging spare sections of track over vulnerable sections of the tank. By the time of Gazala in May 1942 they were also starting a programme of up-gunning their PzKw IIIs and IVs.

* * *

The next British attack, Operation 'Crusader', was launched on 18 November 1941 as a full-blooded attempt to relieve Tobruk. It was initially shrouded by a grandiose programme of deception measures and camouflage. This allowed the 450 tanks of 7th Armd Div to creep secretly into their chosen fighting ground at Gabr Saleh, where they expected Rommel to counter-attack on unfavourable terms to himself. But unfortunately Rommel failed to oblige, for the simple reason that the British deception plan had worked so well that he had not the faintest idea that the main British armoured force was sitting there waiting for him. On 19 November they therefore had to fan out to find him, thereby losing the vital concentration of force that they had achieved at the cost of so much ingenuity and effort. For the next month the battle would consist of a series of confused and fragmented brigade and regimental actions, spread all over the area between Tobruk and the Egyptian frontier wire.

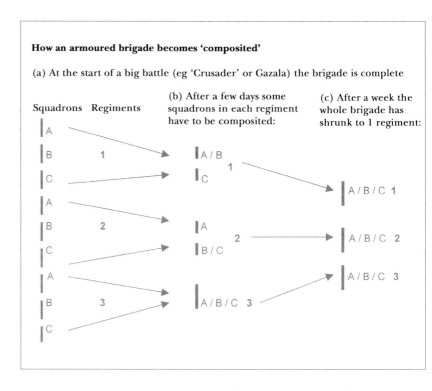

How an armoured brigade becomes 'composited'

(a) At the start of a big battle (eg 'Crusader' or Gazala) the brigade is complete

Squadrons   Regiments

(b) After a few days some squadrons in each regiment have to be composited:

(c) After a week the whole brigade has shrunk to 1 regiment:

A prominent feature of this fighting was the 'fog of war', compounded both by poor radios operating at extreme ranges, and by the high speed of many of the movements. This in turn meant that many of the combats were either entirely unplanned, or planned only at the last moment and with inadequate resources. They became dispersed and uncontrollable, which meant that brigade battles often broke down into scattered regimental, and then squadron fights. After suffering heavy tank losses during the first few days of intense attrition, many regiments would find themselves reduced to squadron strength. Brigades would then have to go into action effectively as regiments and finally, by the end of November, as squadrons. The officers and men would be mixed up between units and put into unfamiliar groupings, so that all continuity of doctrine and tactics was lost.

Eventually both armies effectively ran out of tanks, despite frantic efforts to repair 'crocks' and scour the rear areas for fresh vehicles and crews. Between 18 November 1941 and 15 February 1942 the Germans lost 220 out of 260 tanks (85 per cent); the Italians, 120 out of 154 (78 per cent); and the British, 570 out of 648 (88 per cent). In all cases these figures exclude tanks that were successfully recovered and repaired, so the total number knocked out, before repairs, must have been well over 100 per cent of the starting strength. In human terms, statistically one crew member would be killed, wounded or captured every time a tank was knocked out, although obviously the outcome in any given case might vary between all dying and all escaping unscathed. One officer reported that in a two-day period during the battle of Gazala he commanded no fewer than six different tanks in succession, as each one was shot away beneath him.

(continued on page 41)

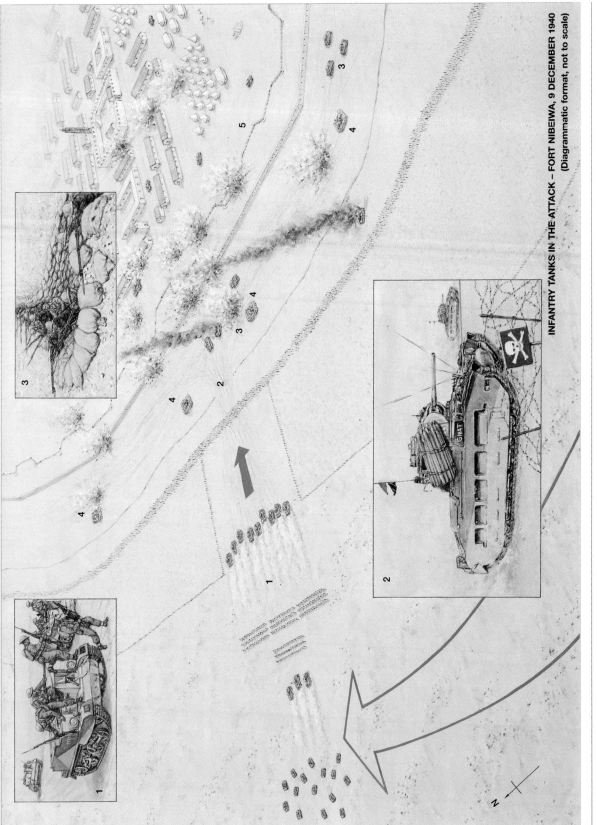

INFANTRY TANKS IN THE ATTACK – FORT NIBEIWA, 9 DECEMBER 1940
(Diagrammatic format, not to scale)

A

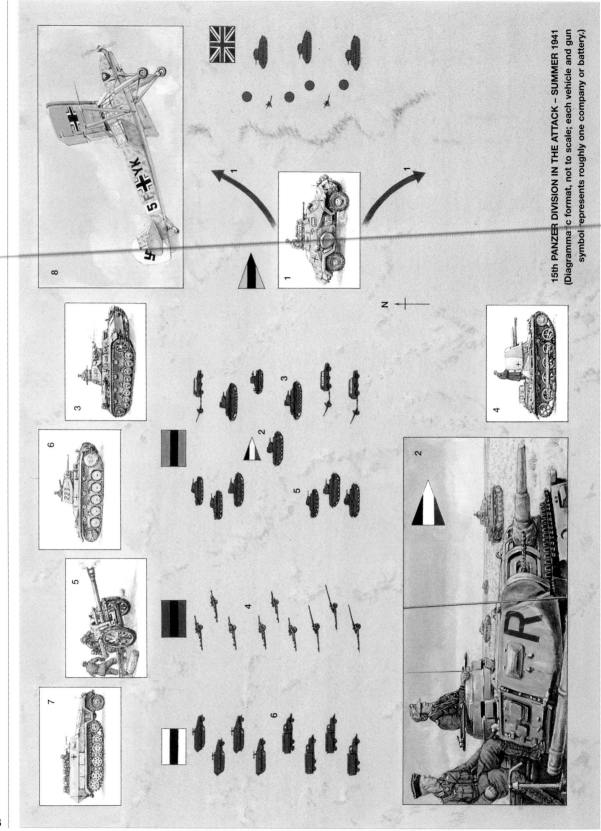

B

15th PANZER DIVISION IN THE ATTACK – SUMMER 1941
(Diagrammatic format, not to scale; each vehicle and gun symbol represents roughly one company or battery.)

N

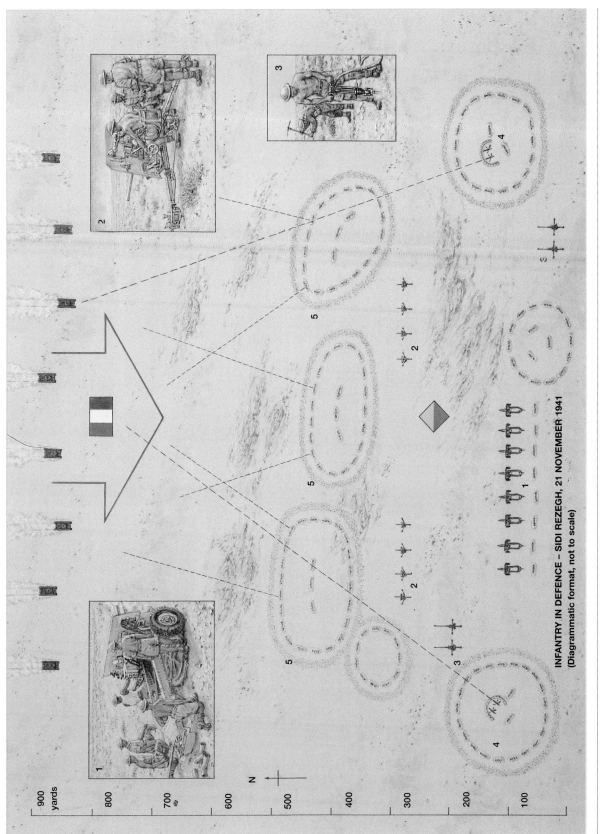

INFANTRY IN DEFENCE – SIDI REZEGH, 21 NOVEMBER 1941
(Diagrammatic format, not to scale)

c

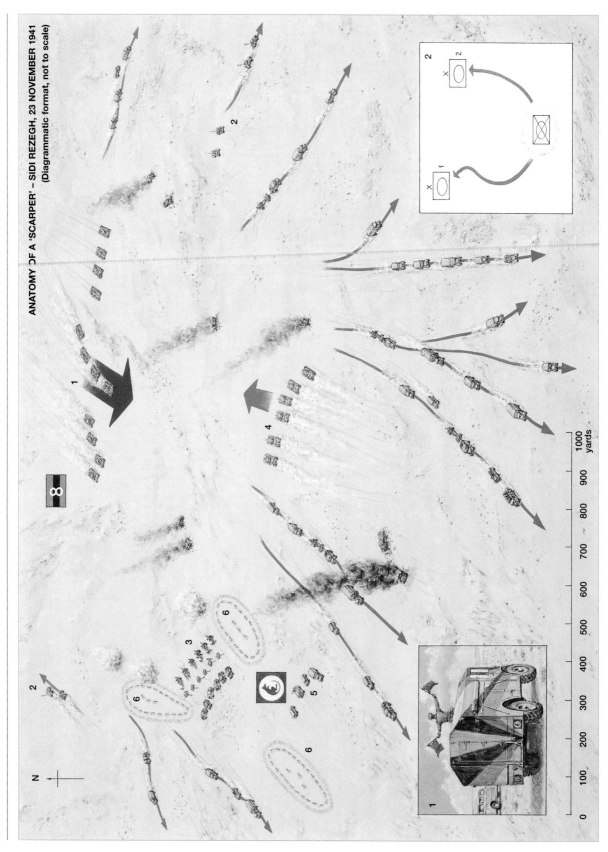

ANATOMY OF A 'SCARPER' – SIDI REZEGH, 23 NOVEMBER 1941
(Diagrammatic format, not to scale)

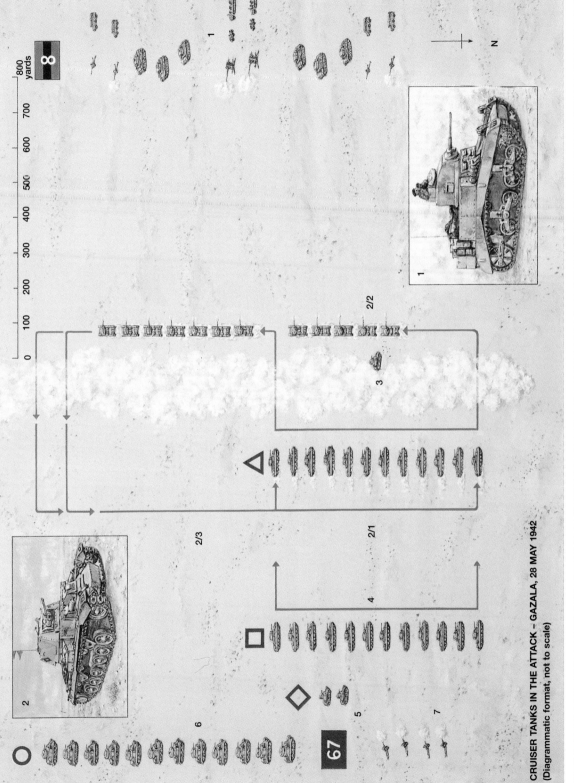

CRUISER TANKS IN THE ATTACK – GAZALA, 28 MAY 1942
(Diagrammatic format, not to scale)

E

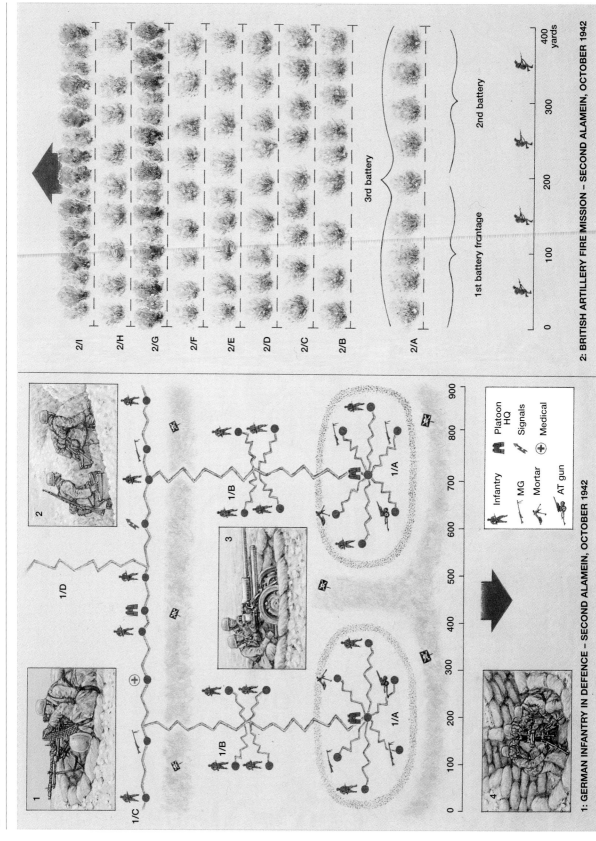

F

1: GERMAN INFANTRY IN DEFENCE – SECOND ALAMEIN, OCTOBER 1942

	Infantry		Platoon HQ		Signals		Medical
	MG		Mortar		AT gun		

2: BRITISH ARTILLERY FIRE MISSION – SECOND ALAMEIN, OCTOBER 1942

2/I
2/H
2/G
2/F
2/E
2/D
2/C
2/B
2/A

3rd battery

2nd battery

1st battery frontage

0   100   200   300   400 yards

1/C
1/D
1/B
1/A

0   100   200   300   400   500   600   700   800   900

BRITISH ARMOUR IN THE PURSUIT – 5 NOVEMBER 1942
7
1
1
2
3
4
4
5
2
3
4
6
86

G

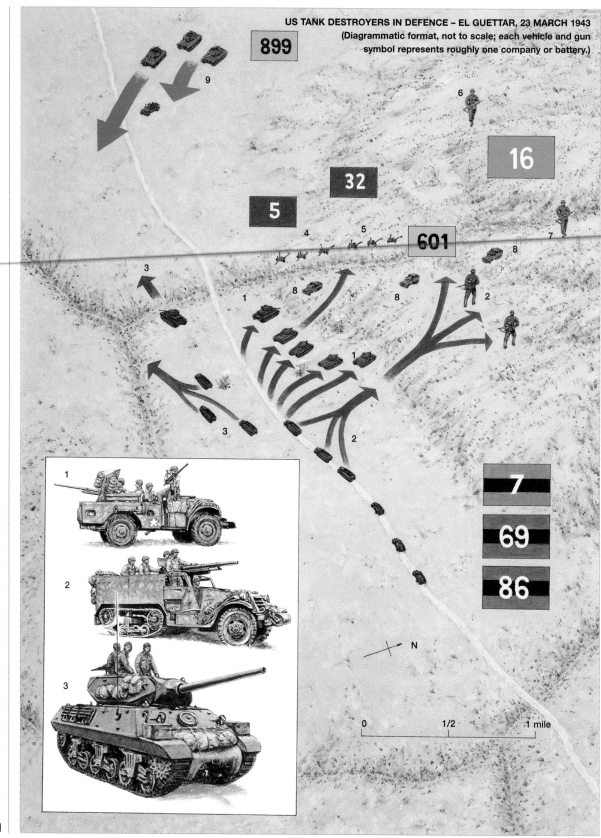

US TANK DESTROYERS IN DEFENCE – EL GUETTAR, 23 MARCH 1943
(Diagrammatic format, not to scale; each vehicle and gun symbol represents roughly one company or battery.)

899

16

32

5

601

7

69

86

N

0   1/2   1 mile

H

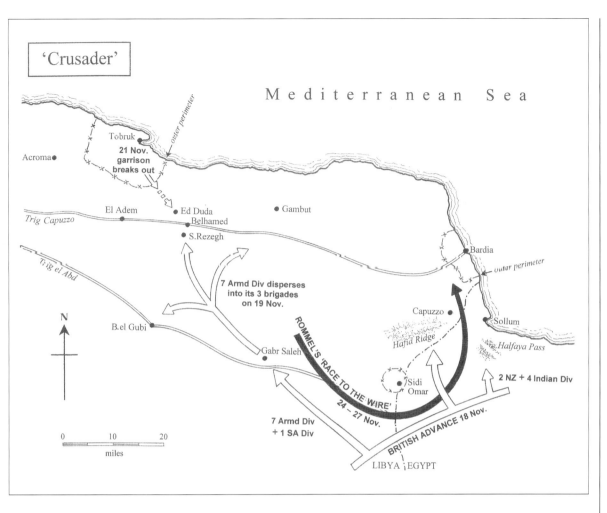

Infantry had a very important role to play in the 'Crusader' fighting, even before the supply of tanks ran out. On the Axis side the Italian infantry divisions had the task of fencing in the Tobruk garrison and stopping its breakout. In the event the successful sortie was itself mainly an infantry and I-tank operation, conducted in a series of short bounds from one enemy post to the next. Meanwhile three British Empire infantry divisions were to press across the frontier into Libya, to pin down the Halfaya defences that had resisted so well in the past, and eventually to invest the fortress of Bardia. At first this was all supposed to be done in a systematic and orderly way, protected on the western flank by 4th Armd Brigade. As the battle developed, however, 7th Armd Div would remorselessly suck the South African and New Zealand infantry, as well as 4th Armd Bde itself, into its own battles around Sidi Rezegh. Nor were there enough resources to stop Axis armour weaving in and out of the British rear areas near the frontier. Time and again an infantry brigade, detached from its division, had to dig in hastily to defend itself against the threat of heavy attacks, which often failed to materialize but which sometimes swept all before them. As in 'Brevity' and 'Battleaxe', the infantry remained nervous about its AT protection, and would continue to clamour for dedicated tank support.

22nd Armd Bde attack at Bir el Gubi, 19 November 1941, in three regimental 'arrowheads'. Each squadron notionally had 16 tanks; Regimental HQs had 4, and Bde HQ, 8 tanks. The brigade was reduced to about half this strength by the Italian 'Ariete' and 'Trieste' Divisions.

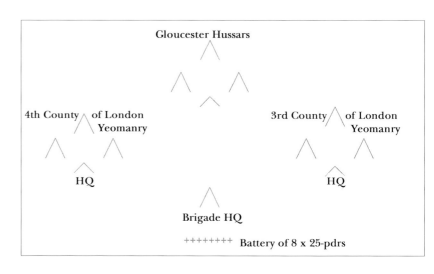

British infantry man a line of two-man 'slits'; although photographed near Bardia in December 1940, this scene is characteristic of the whole campaign. The parapets have been built up with rocks, and note the overhead cover in the foreground. In some rocky areas virtually no digging was possible, and complete stone 'sangars' (an Indian Army term) had to be built above ground level. As so often in all the winter battles in the desert, the men are wearing greatcoats against the cold. (IWM E 1495)

On a very few occasions an enemy attack was so successful that it not only overran an infantry position, but went on to provoke a panic that spread for miles to the rear. The vast scale of the terrain meant that there was always plenty of room for a panicked unit to 'scarper' away into; but in the featureless desert a unit that was driving far and fast might be seen by many others, so the effect could spread far more widely and rapidly than might be the case in other theatres. What tended to happen was that a 'scarper' would spread like wildfire for a few hours, but then die down almost as quickly, with remarkably few human casualties. The cohesion of units might be destroyed for a few days when their vehicles became dispersed or mixed up with other units, but overall it was remarkable how relatively little actual damage was suffered in even the most spectacular panic routs. Perhaps the most striking example of this effect would come on 26–28 June 1942, following the defeat at Mersa Matruh, when Eighth Army somehow managed to extract itself – in chaotic disorder but nevertheless still mostly alive and kicking – back to the Alamein line.

In conclusion, it may be argued that the 'Crusader' battles represented a British victory that in itself was as significant as Second Alamein in late 1942: Rommel's forces were either destroyed or chased away to the west. But the key difference is that in 'Crusader' Eighth Army was unable to sustain its follow-up, mainly for logistic reasons, so it has not been remembered as the success that it actually was.

FROM GAZALA TO ALAMEIN – AND BACK AGAIN

MAY–NOVEMBER 1942

In the immediate aftermath of the 'Crusader' battles the Axis forces withdrew into Tripolitania; but it was not many days before they rebounded and – apparently effortlessly – dispersed the British forces facing them. The inexperienced 22nd Armd Bde was largely destroyed, and in early 1942 the British were forced back into the area of Tobruk. On this occasion, unlike in the spring of 1941, the Tobruk garrison was advanced a few miles towards the west to man the Gazala Line, which embraced a much wider frontage than merely the Tobruk perimeter.

This line consisted of a series of infantry brigade 'boxes', protected by deep minefields in front and massed armoured forces to the rear. However, there were a number of fatal weaknesses in these tactical arrangements. There can be no question that the minefields – probably the thickest ever seen up to that point in the whole of military history – were extremely effective; but the infantry 'boxes' themselves were always vulnerable, under-gunned against tank attack and immobile once their transport was removed to the rear. The whole system also relied heavily upon good, well co-ordinated and strongly concentrated counter-attacks by British tanks which, in the event, signally failed to materialize.

Sheep in wolves' clothing: skilfully modelled and painted drivable dummy Crusader tanks, built of plywood and canvas over light trucks, in order to deceive Axis reconnaissance before the winter 1941/42 offensive; these belonged to the fictitious '101st RTR'. The Germans sometimes fielded similar decoys of their own, but never with anything approaching the British enthusiasm and dedication to this concept. The British also made extensive use of 'wolves in sheeps' clothing' – real tanks disguised as trucks under a discardable canvas 'sunshield' – although British deception measures adopted for Operation 'Crusader' would prove to be too clever by half. (IWM MH 20755)

The British chain of command had one more link – at Eighth Army level – than the Axis forces; they had a much larger army, and needed more extensive staffs. However, despite the frequent disagreements between the Italians and Germans the Axis actually benefited from having two parallel command teams, since each could be smaller and more flexible than the cumbersome British headquarters.

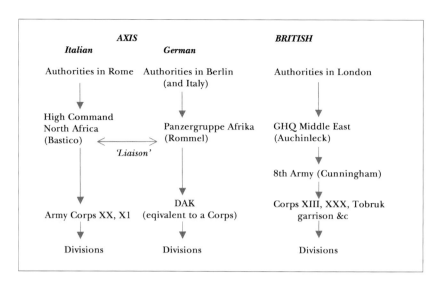

AXIS		**BRITISH**
Italian	*German*	
Authorities in Rome	Authorities in Berlin (and Italy)	Authorities in London
↓	↓	↓
High Command North Africa (Bastico) ←→	Panzergruppe Afrika (Rommel)	GHQ Middle East (Auchinleck)
	'Liaison'	↓
		8th Army (Cunningham)
↓	↓	↓
Army Corps XX, X1	DAK (eqivalent to a Corps)	Corps XIII, XXX, Tobruk garrison &c
↓	↓	↓
Divisions	Divisions	Divisions

The Gazala battle started on 27 May 1942 with a grand, wide-sweeping Axis manoeuvre around the British southern flank (very much in the spirit of Hobart and his British successors). At first the Panzer spearheads made a great impact, and they knocked out a shockingly high proportion of the new M3 Grant tanks, which, along with the new 6-pdr AT guns, had previously been held back as a great British hope. In the event they were consumed in battle almost as quickly as the Cruiser tanks; but they did inflict heavy losses – Rommel would write that 'the advent of the new American tank had torn great holes in our ranks'.

17 February 1942: semaphore flag signal for 'Rally', from an M3 Grant of 5th RTR (note that the commander wears a US crash-helmet supplied with his US tank). Under the right conditions for visibility this old method of communicating could have serious tactical advantages, the most obvious being in cases of radio silence or radio breakdown. The fixed flags flown on radio antennae, in pre-arranged colours and positions of the day, were aids to recognition while still 'turret-down'.

At this date the first 160-odd Grants were still a 'secret weapon'; this photo, showing the detail of its armament, must have been a highly classified document until the enemy actually encountered the type at Gazala, and captured some wrecks. (IWM E 8490)

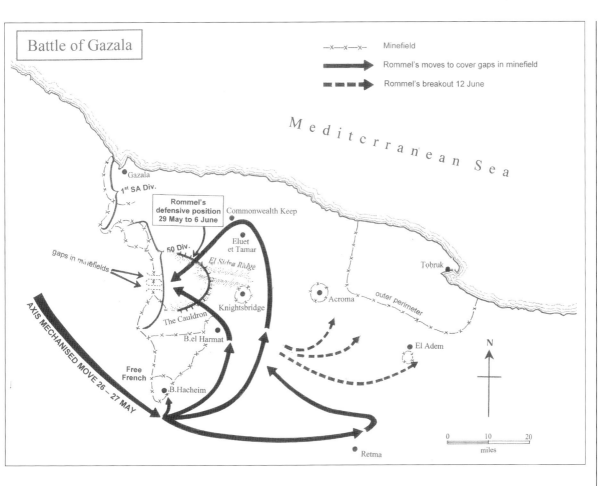

Battle of Gazala

- —x—x—x— Minefield
- ——▶ Rommel's moves to cover gaps in minefield
- ▬ ▬ ▬▶ Rommel's breakout 12 June

Mediterranean Sea

Gazala
1st SA Div.

Rommel's defensive position 29 May to 6 June

Commonwealth Keep

50 Div.

Eluet et Tamar

El Sidra Ridge

gaps in minefields

Tobruk

The Cauldron

Knightsbridge

Acroma

outer perimeter

B.el Harmat

AXIS MECHANISED MOVE 26 – 27 MAY

El Adem

Free French

B.Hacheim

N

0   10   20
miles

Retma

Soon after their initial charge the Axis forces were pushed back against the eastern side of the British minefields, cut off from resupply, where for a few days they were left standing in the open and vulnerable to a crushing counter-attack. In tactical terms this ought to have spelled the end of the Afrika Korps, and many observers recorded their expectant anticipation that the war in Libya was about to be concluded. Alas for such hopes, however, the crushing counter-attack never came.

The nearest approximation to it was Operation 'Aberdeen', which turned out to be a damp squib. This was a disastrous lost opportunity for the British, as they allowed Rommel to open lanes through the minefields and replenish his forces. He was eventually able to brush off the British and pick off their infantry 'boxes' one by one. By 12 June he was able to attack their armour with devastating effect, and by the 20th he had gone the whole way and captured Tobruk itself – the prize that had escaped him throughout 1941. Eighth Army retreated rapidly towards the east, but was promptly bumped out of the Mersa Matruh position in ignominious circumstances, thereafter retiring to Egypt and the Alamein line.

Armour failure, artillery and infantry success
During this time two important tactical developments could be observed. The first was that the British armour had lost its confidence and was becoming combat-shy. It had suffered such crippling losses, and had therefore undergone so many organizational changes, that it

no longer enjoyed any recognizable combat cohesion or ésprit de corps. This was particularly noticeable at Mersa Matruh, where the armour did practically nothing to oppose an Axis force that it outnumbered by at least five to one. Secondly, the British were rediscovering the power of artillery. In the later stages of the 'Crusader' battles they had reverted to artillery-heavy Jock Columns when their armour had been used up. Now, after Gazala and Matruh, they found themselves in a rather similar situation, but this time their response was different. Even before Gazala, Gen Auchinleck had tried to reverse the 'penny-packeting' of armoured brigades, and he was starting to think more in terms of unified armoured divisions fighting together as all-arms groupings. His thinking was not just that a division's support group should be permanently co-located with the armour in a way that had been anathema to Hobart; but also that all the artillery of a division – and preferably of an entire corps – should be concentrated on a single target.

The turning point came on 1 July at Alamein, when Rommel's 90th Light Division ran straight into just such an artillery concentration, laid down by 1st South African Division. The Germans were stopped dead in their tracks in a way that had not been seen since the early days at Gazala. The whole impetus behind Rommel's attack fell away, which gave the British a chance to consolidate their defences, including extensive minefields designed to channel the enemy into prepared killing zones. During a gruelling month of attritional fighting the line was held; but Auchinleck was unable to mount a successful counter-attack at the operational level. There were many examples of good local attacks, especially by infantry at night, but no wider movement to change the higher picture. Churchill (typically) lost patience with his general, and replaced Auchinleck in mid-August, with Gen Alexander as C-in-C Middle East and Gen Montgomery – after the untimely death of the first choice, Gen Gott – at the head of Eighth Army.

Meanwhile, Rommel was regrouping and preparing for a new offensive towards the Alam el Halfa ridge. This blow landed on

Re-ammunitioning a Sherman of 9th Lancers from a supply truck. The Sherman – supplied to this unit of 2nd Armd Bde, 1st Armd Div just in time for Second Alamein – had thicker armour than previous types, a more reliable engine and running gear, and the great tactical advantage of a high mounting for a 75mm all-purpose gun. The harder work of handling the larger and heavier 20lb shells was a light price for the crew to pay, even though the Sherman was designed to carry no fewer than 90 rounds. (Private collection, courtesy Mike Chappell)

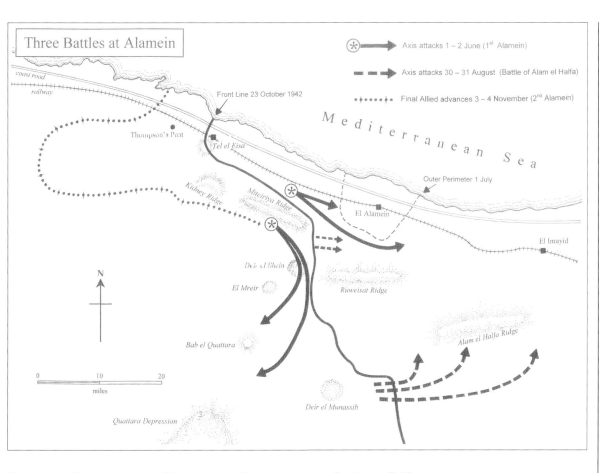

Three Battles at Alamein

Axis attacks 1 – 2 June (1ˢᵗ Alamein)

Axis attacks 30 – 31 August (Battle of Alam el Halfa)

Final Allied advances 3 – 4 November (2ⁿᵈ Alamein)

coast road
railway
Front Line 23 October 1942

Mediterranean Sea

Thompson's Post
Tel el Eisa

Outer Perimeter 1 July

Kidney Ridge
Miteiriya Ridge
El Alamein

El Imayid

N

Deir el Shein
El Mreir
Ruweisat Ridge

Bab el Quattara

Alam el Halfa Ridge

0   10   20
miles

Deir el Munassib

Quattara Depression

31 August; but it was quickly repulsed by a mixture of mines, field artillery, AT guns, and tanks firing from hull-down positions without venturing forward in the 'mobile role'. This was the second British defensive victory in the Alamein area, after which the Axis went entirely onto the defensive themselves.

By this time the British had achieved a number of significant advantages to help them take the offensive. They had finally won command of the air, and also of the air waves: Rommel's excellent radio interception service had been destroyed at First Alamein, while the British equivalent was now making great strides. At the same time there was an unprecedented build-up of infantry, tanks and guns arriving for Eighth Army. Montgomery had already won a reputation during his time at the Staff College for always doubly re-insuring himself against failure in any plan that he made. He was a cautious commander who believed in firepower rather than manoeuvre, and he quickly put an end to all experiments with 'manoeuvre warfare' on the Fuller-Hobart model. His plan for the second battle of Alamein was based on a 'thousand-gun' artillery barrage (actually, fewer than 900 guns), followed up by infantry – essentially the same technique that had been developed in 1917–18 on the Western Front. Tanks were no longer seen as the 'war-winning weapon of the future' but were relegated to a secondary role within the all-arms battle, just as they had been in 1918 – and as they had been within the German Panzer divisions.

The main problem encountered at Second Alamein was the Axis use of mines. At Gazala, First Alamein and Alam el Halfa thick minefields had been an important support for the British, and on this occasion they were a mainstay of Rommel's defence. This in turn meant that the British art of attack suddenly had to be refocused into the art of minefield clearance. Eighth Army's chief engineer, Brig Kisch (who was, incidentally, also one of the fathers of Zionism) found himself the most important man in the army after Montgomery himself. He helped develop a series of new mine-clearing techniques, to improve upon the basic idea of prodding the ground with a bayonet and hoping for the best. One of these was the 'flail tank', which lashed the ground in front of it with rotating chains, to explode mines before the tank itself could be damaged. Another was the electronic (or 'Polish', since it had been invented by a Pole) mine detector, based on detecting variations in the oscillations between two coils, which gave an acoustic signal. Even more important, perhaps, was the new training in minefield discipline, including a standard doctrine for the methodical location, neutralizing, marking and lifting of mines, the marking of cleared lanes, and the subsequent control of traffic within them by Military Police.

In the event the second battle of Alamein went no more smoothly than the first, in the sense that the breakthrough took 12 days to achieve instead of the one day envisaged by Montgomery. The battle of the minefield gaps reached epic proportions, but the armour could not break out on narrow frontages in the face of strong AT defences. Instead, one of the most significant British successes was actually a defensive action, at the 'Snipe' position on 27 October 1942: there 19 of the 6-pdr AT guns, supported by infantry, accounted for more than 50 Axis tanks, while the overwatching British armour did not intervene to any great extent.

Eventually the Axis ran out of resources and pulled out of all their Alamein positions; the Germans left many of their Italian allies with no option but to surrender, by stealing their motor transport. Yet the British pursuit remained lacklustre, and was not helped by heavy rains. At least their Grant and Sherman tanks could fire 75mm HE shells against

A rare view of the wide spacing of British trucks on the march, exactly as required by official tactical doctrine – for armour as much as for soft-skins. The idea was ostensibly to minimize the size of target presented to air attacks, although one suspects that there was also a sub-text related to extending the frontage of any given formation. The photo appears to have been taken from the top of a railway water tower, probably at or somewhere near Alamein in 1942. Note the effect of the wind on the direction of the dust clouds following the two trucks in the background, and the fact that those in the foreground are not raising any dust at all, probably due to subtle differences in the local 'going'.
(Tank Museum 1057/A4)

A Grant advancing, about 55 miles south-east of Tripoli, in late January 1943. This tank is part of the 'South Column' – consisting of 7th Armd Div, 2nd New Zealand Div and 22 Armd Bde – during the pursuit after Second Alamein. It was a movement designed to outflank Axis rearguard positions on the coast, and represented a rare attempt by Montgomery to revert to the sort of mobile warfare that he had condemned in his predecessors. (IWM E 21568)

enemy AT guns, without necessarily needing to call in field artillery support, while this essential capability was still largely unavailable to British-built tanks. Montgomery never did become an expert in the use of armour, in the way that Rommel had been since at least the start of 1940. On the other hand, he was well aware that, for logistical reasons, after both Beda Fomm and 'Crusader' the British pursuits south of Benghazi had been too rushed and therefore too weak in numbers, leaving them too vulnerable to counter-attack. After Second Alamein, Montgomery resolved to go slowly but this time with adequate logistics. In tactical terms it implied an arthritic rate of advance with no spectacular breakthroughs, no lightning manoeuvres and no grand battles of annihilation. The Afrika Korps was left to make a four-month retreat from position to position through Cyrenaica and Tripolitania into southern Tunisia. By February 1943 this withdrawal finally brought it into tactical contact with Gen von Arnim's Fifth Panzer Army, which was already heavily engaged against Gen Clark's Fifth US Army and Gen Anderson's First British Army, both of which had landed in north-west Africa in Operation 'Torch' on 8 November 1942, under overall comand of Gen Eisenhower. Over a wet, cold and miserable winter they had been attempting, without much success, to push eastwards and capture Tunis.

TUNISIA

In mid-February 1943 the Axis launched a major series of counter-attacks for the first time since Alam el Halfa. Thrusting from east to west, von Arnim pushed back the Allies through Faid, Sidi Bou Zid, Sbeitla and Kasserine, while Rommel advanced from the south-east through El Guettar, Gafsa and Feriana. They were hoping to reach either Tebessa or Le Kef – or preferably both. They did score some telling initial successes against green American troops; however, by 22 February they had been ground down to a halt by the Allied defences just north of Kasserine, which enjoyed superior numbers.

49

On 15 February 1943, near Sidi Bou Zid, the US 2/1st Armd Regt attempted to attack a seriously underestimated German force, and ran into a mixed defence of manoeuvring tanks and AT guns in concealed positions. The unit had never seen combat before, and had not trained for tank-vs-tank fighting before embarkation; it simply advanced blindly in a rough V-formation, its speed kicking up considerable dust. The Germans let the leading US tanks pass through the 'PAK-front' before opening fire, and Panzers from 5th and 21st Pz Divs then hit the American flanks; Lt Col Alger's battalion suffered 36 of its 40 Shermans destroyed. (NARA)

Using the advantage of interior lines, Rommel then speedily retired south-westwards to confront his pursuer Montgomery once again, launching a major attack at Medenine on 6 March. But there, as at 'Snipe', the Eighth Army's AT guns (which now included the powerful 17-pdr 'Pheasant') managed to defeat the attack almost unaided. This confirmed not only that AT guns were still the truly decisive weapon of the desert war, but also that the British had at long last understood how to use them properly, at least in defence (although they never did manage to copy the German trick of bringing them forward at the very front of every armoured advance).

After Medenine Montgomery resumed his attack, outflanking the Mareth Line on 20 March, assaulting the Wadi Akarit position on 6 April, and then pursuing far to the north, to Enfidaville. Meanwhile Eisenhower's armies were pressing westwards from Kasserine through Gafsa to El

20 February 1943: US 37mm AT gun north of Kasserine Pass, with German shelling in the distance; this was the day Rommel's force actually captured the pass during its offensive towards Tebessa, although he would be driven out of it again on the 22nd. The towed 37mm AT gun was the same as those mounted in the turrets of Stuart and Grant tanks, and was broadly similar to the obsolescent British 2-pdr. This gun has been sited with some cover from rocks, and shallow slit trenches have been dug as refuges in case the crew come under HE fire. (IWM NA 860)

Early March 1943: the new British 17-pdr (76.2mm, or 3in) AT gun being fired at Medenine, although probably not in anger. The arrival of the 17-pdr at last gave the Allies an AT gun that was almost as good as the German 8.8cm, with the capability to knock out any enemy tank at ranges up to 2,000 yards. The photographer has caught it at full recoil; note the enormous dust clouds thrown up by the high-velocity shock waves – this tended to annoy the infantry that the guns supported, who feared it would pinpoint their position for enemy artillery. Note also that this 'Pheasant' is mounted on a standard 25-pdr carriage, as a stop-gap pending production of a purpose-built version. (IWM NA 1076)

Guettar, and through Sened Station to Maknassy. In April the Allies in northern Tunisia launched a new offensive towards Bizerta, with devastating effect. The Axis forces were increasingly hemmed into a shrinking perimeter around Tunis itself, and increasingly isolated by air power from their logistic base in Sicily. The end came on 13 May, when the last Axis troops finally surrendered.

In tactical terms the Tunisian campaign represented a startling mixture of the ancient with the ultra-modern. Because the terrain was so rugged and mountainous, where few motor vehicles could venture far from the valley floors, a new window of opportunity was opened for transport by mules (the French even managed to field some horsed cavalry). Yet at the same time this campaign saw the first use of the redoubtable PzKw VI Tiger heavy tank, on 28 November 1942. It was extremely heavily armoured and carried essentially the same 8.8cm AT gun that in its towed version had

---

Independent Tank Destroyer Battalion

(intended to be attached to armoured divisions, but in practice sometimes attached to infantry divisions)

Organization of 8 June 1942:

```
                    ┌─────────┐
                    │ HQ Coy  │
                    └─────────┘
   ┌──────────┐  ┌──────────┐  ┌──────────┐  ┌──────────┐
   │    ⬭     │  │    ⬭     │  │    ⬭     │  │    ╱     │
   └──────────┘  └──────────┘  └──────────┘  └──────────┘
    TD Coy A      TD Coy B      TD Coy C      Recce Coy
```

Each TD coy has 4 x M6 37mm portees + 8 x M3 75mm   *11 x light armour*
halftracks   *+ jeeps & m/cycles*

(In the reorganization of 27 January 1943, all the M6 and M3 improvised TDs were replaced by purpose-built M10 tracked SP guns.)

already proved itself lethally effective against Allied armour. However, on 28 November only four Tigers were committed to combat, and they did not do particularly well. They were later joined by only 22 others, which total had shrunk to just eight by April 1943. They were mechanically unreliable, and their main weak spot was their tracks and running gear which, if damaged by mines or gunfire, could be repaired only if the Germans continued to control the battlefield overnight – a luxury upon which they could no longer count. The new heavier Allied AT guns could also deliver shrewd blows from flank or rear especially when – as was often the case in Tunisia – the Tigers were exposed by leading the attack into enemy defensive positions.

On 14 February 1943 the Tigers were joined by the novel *Nebelwerfer* six-barrelled rocket projector ('Screaming Meemie' or 'Moaning Minnie' to the cursing Allied troops). By 1944 both of these weapon systems would grow to be an absolute scourge of the Allied armies, but in early 1943 they were neither mature nor numerous enough to affect the course of the battle significantly.

Another tactical innovation was the US 'Tank Destroyer' concept. Like the British with I-tanks and the Germans with PzKw IVs, the Americans quite rightly regarded their heavier (technically, 'medium') tanks as a suitable auxiliary for infantry operations. But when it came to fighting a 'tank battle' they had invented a whole new class of vehicle that they called tank destroyers, presumably intended to do the job of British Cruisers or German PzKw IIIs in the tank-killing role. In early 1943 these specialized battalions were still in transition between three types of equipment, two of them inadequate: the unarmoured M6 truck carrying a 37mm AT gun as a portee; the lightly armoured M3 halftrack mounting an old 75mm field gun; and the purpose-built M10, based on a Sherman

23 March 1943, near El Guettar: officers of the US 601st TD Bn confer next to an M3 command halftrack. In the background is one of the unit's 75mm GMC tank destroyers that played a critical role that day in resisting Kampfgruppe von Broich – see Plate H. The jeep – also supplied in large numbers to the British during 1942 – was at this date part of the tactical equipment of each TD battalion's reconnaissance company; each platoon had five MG-armed jeeps and two armoured cars. (NARA)

tank chassis, with a topless turret for a powerful 3in (76.2mm) AT gun. The common theme with all these vehicles was that their armour – if any – was relatively poor, but in the right circumstances their firepower was supposed to be relatively effective against enemy tanks.

The tank destroyer concept relied upon the odd tactical idea that in battle a commander would have the time and means available to select the perfect counter for a given threat. Moreover, for two years in the desert the British had been cursing any of their tanks – including their US-built M3 Stuarts – that they perceived to have thin armour protection, and their experiments with portee AT guns had been notably unsuccessful. Neither type of vehicle had really been capable of supporting the sort of 'tank-vs-tank battles' that they thought they were fighting, and they were doubtless surprised that their new allies hoped to fight similar battles with even lighter vehicles. However, terrain was also a factor: in Egypt and Libya there had often been hugely wide fields of fire, where soft- or thin-skinned vehicles could be picked off at ranges well over 1,000 yards, while the hills and vegetation of Tunisia offered many more opportunities for TDs to 'ambush' enemy AFVs from cover at closer ranges. As the US Official History somewhat coyly put it (pages 672–673): 'Experience demonstrated that [the TDs] could not be used to "hunt tanks", since in a fire fight with tanks they soon succumbed. Their mobility was chiefly useful to avoid hostile fire or to get in a better firing position.' When translated, this seems to mean that they were best used in hull-down positions or exploiting cover. Remarkably, therefore, the TD concept actually survived the test of battle in the Tunisian hills, and at El Guettar it was even seen as a success. The M10 Wolverine was not nearly as fast as the 37mm portee or 75mm halftrack, but it was better armoured and much better armed than the latter; it would continue in Allied service in various forms throughout the rest of the war, though the doctrine for its employment would be less rigidly defined.

Valentine tanks carrying Scottish infantry north of Gabés on 1 March 1943, apparently at a scale of one platoon per four tanks. Not visible in this photo is the fact that some of the tanks are towing AT guns – thus apparently creating a remarkable 'all arms' force for this low down in the chain of command. It is clear, however, that this is a totally staged scene. The tanks are closed up track to track; the infantry present sitting ducks for enemy machine guns; and it is ridiculous to tow AT guns into battle behind tanks, since they always need to act independently, with their own dedicated vehicles carrying crew and ammunition. (IWM NA 1672)

12 March 1943: British infantry advancing through taped gaps in a minefield. The process of gapping minefields did not stop when the mines had been detected and lifted: the cleared lane also had to be mapped, marked and policed. In this case the gap is wide enough for two-way infantry traffic but only one tank; unless there was a second gap nearby to accommodate vehicles returning to the rear, some system would be required for the Military Police to control the flow according to higher command's tactical needs at a given moment. (IWM NA 1152)

Lessons of Tunisia

The US Official History provides a list of the other tactical lessons that the American army learned in Tunisia. In essence these were the same ones that had emerged from the Great War, and which had been re-learned by the British in their desert campaigns of 1940–42. In fact, the first few harked back even further, to the Victorian verities of the North-West Frontier or the Boer War – such timeless principles as securing the high ground, and the need for infantry to scout, patrol and learn to read maps. Beyond these there were some sound basic axioms (although they seem not to have been obvious to Fuller or Hobart in the 1930s) about the need to co-ordinate all arms and to use infantry in close proximity to tanks. There was also a need to keep armour concentrated on a narrow front rather than dispersed or 'penny-packeted', which had of course been a major difference between German and British practice in 1941. Then there was the need for depth in defence; for infantry to hug the creeping barrage in the attack; and for everyone to spend time in preparation and rehearsal before launching any attack.

The US Official History goes on to make the fundamental point that officers must be competent – perhaps a sideswipe at some of their individual commanders who had reacted badly to the German thrust towards Kasserine. It is obviously unavoidable that at the start of any war armies will tend to bring a relatively high proportion of peacetime officers into the front line, alongside the true warrior types who will gradually rise to the top in later days. However, in this case there was also a hint that doctrine had demanded headquarters to be located too far behind the front line, making it difficult to maintain full control over the fighting.

At this stage of the war the Germans had come to realize not only that they were outnumbered and outgunned, but that this was true to such an extent that most of their old assumptions about tactics were out of date. Already at Second Alamein in October 1942 the weight of Montgomery's air power and artillery had left them all too little room for manoeuvre; there had been no new 'race to the wire' such as Rommel had mounted a few days into the 'Crusader' battles of November 1941. In Tunisia in 1943 they were confronted by two brand new armies coming in from the west, including an American one that could deploy apparently unlimited scales of equipment. The weight of its air and artillery support was particularly crushing, especially since the Luftwaffe had been disastrously weakened. In these circumstances German tactical analysts might growl resentfully that US tactics were 'inflexible, plodding and all about material superiority' (exactly like Montgomery's, in effect); but the fact remained that the Germans could not win such a battle.

FURTHER READING

J.A.I. Agar-Hamilton & L.C.F. Turner, *Crisis in the Desert, May–June 1942* (Oxford UP, Cape Town 1952)

J.A.I. Agar-Hamilton & L.C.F. Turner, *The Sidi Rezeg Battles* (Oxford UP, Cape Town 1957)

Niall Barr, *Pendulum of War, the Three Battles of Alamein* (Cape, London 2004). Probably the definitive history of these battles for our generation.

Peter Beale, *Death by Design, British Tank development in the Second World War* (Sutton, Stroud 1998)

Shelford Bidwell & Dominick Graham, *Firepower, British Army Weapons and Theories of War, 1904–45* (George Allen & Unwin, London 1982)

Michael Carver, *El Alamein* (Batsford, London 1962)

Michael Carver, *Tobruk* (Pan, London 1964)

Michael Carver, *Dilemmas of the Desert War* (Batsford, London 1986)

Keith Douglas, *Alamein to Zem Zem* (PL Poetry, London 1946; Bantam Books, October 1985). The elegant autobiography of a tank commander-poet.

David French, 'The Desert War, 1940–42' in *Raising Churchill's Army* (Oxford UP, Oxford 2000), pp.212–239

Paddy Griffith, 'British Armoured Warfare in the Western Desert, 1940–43' in J.P. Harris & F.H. Toase (eds), *Armoured Warfare* (Batsford, London 1990)

Men of 9th Bn Durham Light Infantry re-enact for the photographer their capture of a concrete bunker in the Mareth Line on 12 April 1943. Such massive structures had never before been encountered in North Africa, and would not be again once the Mareth position had been carried. (IWM NA 2173)

J.P. Harris, *Men, Ideas and Tanks, British Military Thought and Armoured Forces, 1903–39* (Manchester UP, 1995)

George F. Howe, *Northwest Africa: Seizing the initiative in the West* (US Army Official History, Washington DC 1957)

Thomas L. Jentz, *Tank Combat in North Africa, The Opening Rounds, February–June 1941* (Schiffer, Atglen PA 1998)

B.H. Liddell Hart (ed), *The Rommel Papers* (Collins, London 1953)

Fred Majdaleny, *Patrol* (Longman & Green, London 1953). Classic novel of British infantry in Tunisia.

Bryan Perrett, *Through Mud & Blood* (Robert Hale, London 1975). The I-tanks.

PLATE COMMENTARIES

A: INFANTRY TANKS IN THE ATTACK – FORT NIBEIWA, 9 DECEMBER 1940

(Diagrammatic format, not to scale)

By December 1940 the Italians had established themselves in a series of forts near Sidi Barrani (60 miles inside Egypt, so nominally in British-controlled territory), as a preliminary to an intended thrust at Alexandria and Cairo. Over a period of nearly four months they had built up their forts as much as their limited logistic resources allowed, and protected them with dug-outs, trenches, sangars (piled stone parapets), wire, mines and (uncompleted) AT ditches. At Fort Nibeiwa their garrison consisted of Group Maletti, which comprised infantry, field artillery, AT guns and transport, as well as a few armoured cars and M11 light tanks. Overall in the theatre the Italians outnumbered the British by about 5:1 in troops, and they enjoyed superior air power.

The British, however, had some important advantages of their own. They were operating close to their logistic base and initially with adequate motor transport. They also had a whole well-trained armoured division, which was far superior to the few tanks the Italians had available – in particular, a 'secret weapon' in the shape of the Matilda Mk II infantry tank, which proved to be impenetrable by any Italian weapon. Thirdly, they held the advantage of surprise when they launched their attack on 9 December. At Nibeiwa they were able to exploit this because they had previously spotted a gap in the minefield to the rear (western side) of the fort, which had been left open to allow access for Italian transport.

By a silent night march they manoeuvred to the rear of the fort, and at 7am they unleashed an artillery and MG bombardment on identified defensive positions. Fifteen minutes later they charged in with tanks through the unmined gap, initially with a squadron in the first line, immediately followed by infantry. There followed two and a half hours of very fierce fighting – first against the Italian tanks, though not all of these could be manned in time, and then around the Italian artillery sangars. The garrison's resistance was patchy, although their commander, Gen Maletti, died bravely firing a machine gun. The British captured the fort, while their tanks went onwards to their 'forward rally'.

A1: After their surprise night march around from the south, Matildas of A Sqn, 7th RTR, followed by motor infantry of 2nd Bn Queen's Own Cameron Highlanders, turned through 180 degrees. The infantry debussed from their Universal ('Bren gun') carriers **(inset 1)**, well short of the objective (given their unimpressive troop-carrying capacity and armour); then the whole force lunged through the minefield gap and thin wire obstacles to assault the fort. A tank battalion was supposed to consist of a headquarters element with four tanks, and three squadrons each of four troops of four tanks – a total of 16 tanks per squadron, to make 52 per battalion.

A2: The uncompleted AT ditch; in the event it proved to be relatively easy to cross, although the British had over-prepared by attaching fascines – awkwardly – to the turrets of the Matilda Mk II tanks **(inset 2)**; this experiment was not repeated. The Matilda was deemed to be too slow for British armoured divisions, but its heavy armour would quickly come to be admired by all the desert armies of 1940–41; at Nibeiwa, Italian AP shot glanced off its glacis plate and turret.

A3: M11 light tanks of the Italian 2nd Bn, 4th Tank Regt attempted to resist, but were quickly swept away.

A4: The Italian artillery sangars had to be knocked out one by one; their crews resisted bravely until overrun.

A5: The Italian infantry positions **(inset 3)** inside the masonry perimeter wall came under suppressive fire from the British artillery; they were quickly overrun thereafter.

B: 15th PANZER DIVISION IN THE ATTACK – SUMMER 1941

(Diagrammatic format, not to scale; each vehicle and gun symbol represents roughly one company or battery.)

By contrast to the Fuller-Hobart theory of armoured warfare, which stressed high speed and dispersion, the

Panzer division in fact moved relatively slowly, in order to keep fairly closely grouped as an all-arms force. The systematic, deliberate approach assisted command and control; importantly, it also allowed the concentration of firepower against a single chosen spot. This diagram illustrates a 'generic' action:

B1: When the division was on the move it would be preceded to front and flanks by a screen of the motorcycles, armoured cars and light tanks of Recce Unit 33; **(inset 1)** shows an SdKfz 222 light armoured car. Their task was to locate the enemy and maintain a constant stream of reports upon which the divisional commander could make his plans. Depending on the circumstances he might then decide to engage, or to turn away; in any case, at certain times of day the division would halt to close up, replenish and take stock, which could impose significant delays on any planned combat actions.

(Inset 2) PzKw III Befehlswagen command tank of GenMaj Neumann-Silkow, GOC 15th Pz Div (until he was killed by shellfire on 6 December 1941), 'leading from the front'. These vehicles had a fake wooden gun and mantlet to allow more room for extra radios and other command equipment. Photos show Neumann-Silkow using one marked with the 'R' of Pz Regt 8's regimental staff.

B2: Assuming the divisional commander decided to press on, he would initiate the long-range firepower phase. This meant bringing forward his front line of armour and AT guns **(B3)** to about 2,000 yards from the enemy – beyond the range of enemy AT guns, which could normally reach little further than 800 yards. The PzKw IVs, issued to the 4th and 8th Cos of the Panzer regiment **(inset 3)**, would bombard the enemy with HE shells; meanwhile cover against counter-attack was provided by the towed AT guns – and the few self-propelled Panzerjäger I tank destroyers then available **(inset 4)** – of Motorized AT Unit 33. This was co-ordinated with a bombardment by

B4: The 10.5cm **(inset 5)** and 15cm field guns of Artillery Regt 33. The general aim was to suppress enemy AT guns and infantry, or even persuade the enemy force to withdraw. If the enemy remained in place, the divisional commander reconsidered his options based on reconnaissance reports – and the evidence of his own eyes. If the bombardment seemed to have damaged the enemy badly and – crucially – had neutralized most of his AT guns, then a full-blown assault might be attempted. Even then, however, few commanders would wish to launch an assault unless there were wider general or operational reasons for doing so. In practice it is striking how cautious the Germans showed themselves to be in this respect, and a majority of bombardments were not followed up. If an assault actually was ordered, it would be led by

B5: The tanks of Pz Regt 8. At this date each battalion still had one or two companies equipped with the light PzKw II **(inset 6)** alongside its PzKw IIIs; the light tanks would be relegated to reconnaissance duties as soon as they could be replaced with more mediums. The tanks would pace through and be closely followed by the towed AT guns and PzKw IVs in the advanced line. As it reached the enemy this force would engage the enemy tanks and AT guns, probably at ranges of 600–800 yards and predominantly with AP shot.

B6: If the action was successful, the truck- and halftrack-borne infantry of Motorized Inf Regt 115 or 200 would arrive quickly to capture, occupy and mop up the whole depth of the objective. **(Inset 7)** There were never enough of the superior SdKfz 251 halftracks – which carried a complete infantry section – to equip more than, at most, one of the regiment's battalions. The rest travelled in trucks, of many different German and captured models.

(Inset 8) Rommel's personal Fiesler Fi156 Storch, 5F+YK, was made available by Recce Squadron 2(H)/14. At the height of any battle there was a good chance that the army commander himself might drop in – presumably to the irritation of the local commander, but also hopefully to impose an operational view on minor tactics.

German SdKfz 251 command halftrack of a divisional staff, identified not only by the tin pennant – see Plate B2 – but also by the large aerial of its special radio equipment. The field telephone cable leading off to bottom left implies that there is at least one more HQ staff team near at hand, in close (and radio-secure) communication. (Private collection)

Stowage racks for 7.5cm shells in the deceptively spacious-looking fighting compartment of a PzKw IV; normally about 80 shells of three natures (HE, AP and smoke) could be carried in each tank – compared with only 48 carried by the British Grant. Before the arrival in August 1942 of the Ausf F2 model with a long 7.5cm L/43 AT gun, the PzKw IV was optimized for firing HE to suppress infantry and AT guns – see Plate B inset 3; in British terminology, the earlier models were 'I-tanks'. (Tank Museum 2371/D2)

C: BRITISH INFANTRY IN DEFENCE – SIDI REZEGH, 21 NOVEMBER 1941

(Diagrammatic format, not to scale)

Throughout 1941 and most of 1942 a major weakness in British operations was the lurking fear among their infantry that they lacked adequate means of defence against tanks. In part this was a psychological effect of the Dunkirk campaign; but it was also based on their knowledge that the AT weapons available to them were generally less than devastating.

Theoretically, an infantry division was supposed to be self-defending against tanks, based on its four types of AT weapon. The Boys AT rifle could (unexpectedly) be effective against the lightest tanks (Italian M11, German PzKw I & II), but it did not inspire confidence. There was certainly a perception that some more powerful hand-portable weapon was required, but this would not appear until well into 1943, in the form of the PIAT. The 2-pdr AT gun, which could be effective against all tanks in the field in 1941, was an excellent purpose-built weapon, but was increasingly becoming obsolete. The 40mm Bofors light AA gun used in the AT role would normally only be brought into action in a 'last ditch' situation (this was even more true of the superlative 3.7in AA gun). Finally, the 25-pdr gun-howitzer of the field artillery regiments was – despite its relatively low muzzle velocity – genuinely useful in the AT role.

There were many and varied problems with each of these elements, not least the fact that both the Bofors and the 25-pdr were dual-purpose weapons: if they were shooting at tanks they could not be performing their primary roles. Ideally all this would be supplemented by provision of I-tanks at a scale of one 'army tank brigade' per infantry division, or one I-tank regiment per infantry brigade; but in practice this support was not always forthcoming, and the infantry usually felt they were left far too short of tank support. However, this was not the whole picture, since the historical record shows many instances when Axis armour was indeed beaten off – sometimes even when it tried to make an assault to close

quarters. This diagram of an action during the 'Crusader' battles is an example, notionally showing part of 5th South African Bde south of Sidi Rezegh airfield, with support from 9th SA Field Battery and 3rd SA AT Battery. That day the South Africans successfully beat off a number of probes by German and Italian armour, and destroyed seven tanks – so obviously the anti-tank glass could be 'half full' as much as it could be 'half empty'.

As for infantry defence against enemy infantry and artillery, the idea was to dig in for all-round defence in essentially the same way as it would in Europe, calling on mortars and supporting artillery to boost the firepower of its own rifles, grenades and machine guns. Interlocking fields of fire would be arranged, especially for Vickers machine guns and, to a lesser extent, Bren LMGs. However, in the desert the essential – but high-silhouette – transport vehicles had nowhere to hide from enemy fire unless deep pits were laboriously dug for them; so more normally they would stay miles behind the fighting positions by day, and come back only at night. At Gazala in May–June 1942 the infantry brigade 'boxes' would also be spaced so far apart that they were unable to support each other effectively, so they could be picked off one by one. This was doubly damaging, since the foot soldiers would then often find themselves stranded without transport on which to escape.

C1: 8 x 25-pdrs of 9th SA Field Battery firing in the AT role **(inset 1)**.

C2: 8 x 2-pdr AT guns of 3rd SA Anti-Tank Battery **(inset 2)**.

C3: 4 x Bofors AA guns of 5th SA Division Light AA Regt, deployed for use in the AT role.

C4: 4 x Vickers MMGs of an infantry unit's support company, firing on pre-planned lines from infantry positions.

C5: Infantry platoon positions, including Bren gun fires. Each platoon has a rough oval of slit trenches with an HQ element in the centre, and company HQ is placed slightly behind to observe and control – by means of message runners, since only enough radios were available for liaison with battalion HQ. Barbed wire protection would usually be difficult enough to arrange in a mobile battle, and organizing minefields would take much longer still.

(Inset 3) It was never very difficult to dig into sand or soft earth, but in a rather large proportion of the desert terrain the sand had been blown or washed away from the bedrock, so infantry would face major problems creating even a shallow 'shell scrape'. In such defensive positions slit trenches had to be excavated by sappers using pneumatic drills and explosives.

D: ANATOMY OF A 'SCARPER' – SIDI REZEGH, 23 NOVEMBER 1941

(Diagrammatic format, not to scale)

The psychological frailty of Allied infantry when facing enemy armoured attacks could be multiplied several times over if it infected their supporting transport drivers on a day of crisis. On such occasions a major stampede or 'scarper' might result; other sarcastic names for this phenomenon included 'flap', 'gold rush', or to racing enthusiasts 'The Msus Stakes' and 'The Gazala Gallop'. More officially, the 7th Armd Div debrief described this particular episode as 'an unnecessarily rapid movement of transport'. There were numerous other examples, especially when the infantry defences were actually dented by the enemy or (perhaps even more frighteningly) outflanked.

Pictured here is an incident on what the Germans called 'Totensonntag', two days after the loss of Sidi Rezegh airfield on 21 November, when large numbers of soft-skinned vehicles from 7th Armd Div's and 5th SA Bde's transport echelons were outflanked and surprised by elements of 15th Panzer Division. The debacle was the fault of poor British intelligence as to the enemy's status and intentions, compounded by unrealistically high command expectations of how quickly their own forces could consolidate a powerful defensive position. This highlights the particularly thick fog of war in which the 'Crusader' battles were fought (but which also hovered to some degree over all the other desert battles).

D1: An unexpected attack by Pz Regt 8 appeared from the north-east – the very direction from which New Zealand reinforcements had been expected. In the face of the Panzers the transport fled wildly across the desert in all directions. In a typical 'scarper' every type of vehicle would be represented: field cars, shooting brakes, small trucks, medium trucks, heavy trucks, ambulances, gun tractors (with or without their guns) and recovery vehicles. Their drivers would be disorientated, and when – as in this case – the enemy was firing effectively at some of them, they would verge on a state of panic. Individual drivers might pick up fugitives and survivors from broken vehicles, to the point when their own trucks became overloaded and so broke down in turn. In general, however, a surprisingly high proportion of them would get away unscathed.

D2: As the transport fled, the enemy's progress was meanwhile being observed from the flanks by South African armoured cars, and opposed frontally by whatever few 'teeth' arm elements could be collected. These consisted mainly of

D3: Some obsolete South African 18-pdr field guns, a few 2-pdr AT guns, and

D4: Some Crusader tanks. These were all collected up and led towards the enemy by

D5: Brig 'Jock' Campbell, now commanding 7th Support Group, who advanced against the flood with a few of his staff.

Sollum, 21 April 1941: Coldstream Guardsman using a field telephone from his meticulously dug slit trench, complete with an elbow-shelf at the lip and spoil thrown up front and back. Such trenches gave almost complete safety from mortar and shell fire, unless they suffered a direct hit (see Plate C5). Telephone cable was frequently cut, however, by fire and by passing vehicles. Note that even in April the morning temperature is still too cold for him to shed his greatcoat and 'cap comforter'. (IWM E 2554)

(Inset 1) Honour on this occasion was saved by the personal example and leadership of the legendary 'Jock' Campbell, VC. Riding in the roof hatch of his armoured command vehicle (which he insisted should move at no more than 8mph, despite its driver's inclination to go very much faster), he tried to rally vehicles and guns to face the advancing Panzers by means of improvised blue and red flags.

D6: There were also some infantry positions of 7th Support Group.

This plate shows the early phase of such an event, while the enemy is still in presence: but what it cannot show are the three or four days that would follow, during which the scattered drivers and vehicles all had to recover, sort themselves out and find their parent units. In the vastness of the desert this could be a very long process, so the overall disruption to the fighting capabilities of the army could be enormously greater than might be implied by the short final casualty list.

(Inset 2) Brig Campbell's 7th Support Group consisted of most of the artillery and infantry of 7th Armoured Division. In prewar theory this was intended to be semi-detached from the division's two (later, three) armoured brigades; it was relegated to the static role of securing a base or 'harbour' upon which the tanks could fall back to leaguer, rather than manoeuvring alongside them. On 23 November 1941 this doctrine had the unfortunate effect that the Support Group was left high and dry, with much of its motor transport unprotected, while most of the tanks were elsewhere.

59

Le Kef, Tunisia, 12 February 1943: Crusader tank of First Army testing 6-pdr smoke shell – see Plate E. Ever since 1916 British tacticians had set great store by smoke, and in North Africa they had practised with it rather more often than they were able to use it in combat. Before the arival of the Grant tank in spring 1942 it usually had to be fired from field artillery, but smoke shells would become increasingly available for tanks from mid 1942 onwards. The sporting cry of 'Two up and bags of smoke!' (i.e. two units forward, one in support) would only increase its hold upon the British military imagination thereafter. (IWM NA 785)

E: CRUISER TANKS IN THE ATTACK – GAZALA, 28 MAY 1942

(Diagrammatic format, not to scale)

On the first day of the battle of Gazala the British were surprised by Rommel's wide sweep around their southern flank. A series of disconnected combats were fought over the following 48 hours, in which both sides lost heavily but the initial confusion was only partially clarified. One of these actions involved the British 2nd Armd Bde facing 15th Pz Div; and as part of this the 10th Hussars made some squadron attacks according to the tactics (shown here) that they had carefully rehearsed during the previous few weeks.

The basic thinking was that German AT weapons could be lethal at ranges up to 2,000 yards, whereas the British could knock out the German tanks only at about 600 yards; the problem was therefore to cross the intervening ground unscathed. The chosen solution was to use artillery to lay down a smokescreen at 600 yards from the enemy, to cover the approach march of the British tanks in line abreast. These would then pop out of the smoke at their ideal tactical range from the enemy, and then turn 90 degrees into line ahead, firing 'broadsides' on the move. With this simultaneous concentration of a whole squadron's firepower, it was hoped that the 'tank battle' would be won. If it was not, then the squadron would not charge forward recklessly in the bad old 'Balaklavering' manner, but would go back into the smoke, return to its starting position, and repeat the procedure. Meanwhile the next squadron behind them would be doing the same thing, following in their footsteps, and this caracole would continue until replenishment was needed.

There were arguably three weaknesses in this idea. The first was that the artillery that was being used to lay down smoke would not be available to suppress the enemy AT guns with HE. As in previous British battles, the armoured brigades did not have enough artillery available for that task, whereas the Germans usually managed to arrange better concentrations of firepower. Secondly, the concept of firing on the move was itself suspect. For a number of reasons the British armour continued to believe in it and train for it; but it was surely axiomatic that it was easier to aim accurately from a stationary tank rather than a moving one. Finally, moving in a line that presented each tank's flank and running gear to the enemy, rather than its frontal armour, was also dangerous – especially if the targets were being silhouetted in front of a smokescreen at the time, like a line of ducks in a fairground shooting gallery.

E1: Tanks and AT guns of 15th Pz Div, including some 8.8cm.

E2: The Crusaders of A Sqn 10th Hussars approach in line abreast (E2/1); pass through the smokescreen, then turn 90° to fire to the flank while on the move in line ahead (E2/2). They then make two more 90° turns to return through the smoke and pass back towards the start line (E2/3).

E3: RHA observer in a Stuart tank, directing artillery fire onto the enemy from a position in the forward edge of the smoke screen **(inset 1)**.

E4: The Crusaders of B Sqn 10th Hussars approach, ready to follow A Sqn through the smokescreen.

E5: Regimental HQ of 10th Hussars, in Stuarts; the blue flag bears the white '67' of the regiment's tactical serial number.

E6: The Grants of C Sqn 10th Hussars, held back as a heavy reserve.

E7: 25-pdrs of the RHA firing smoke shell to maintain the smokescreen, and HE to suppress the enemy.

(Inset 2) A9 Cruiser, 1941. Before the arrival of the Grant such close-support tanks were the only types in Eighth Army that had been capable of firing HE; unfortunately they were extremely few in number.

F1: GERMAN INFANTRY IN DEFENCE – SECOND ALAMEIN, OCTOBER 1942

The second battle of Alamein consisted of a series of attacks by Eighth Army against pre-prepared Axis defences. Most of the time this battle was fought between infantry, artillery and mine warfare troops. The armour on each side normally played only a secondary role, and found it difficult to make headway not only through the minefields, but also against very effective screens of AT guns. The key to the Axis defences was the way they laid out their infantry and its supports. Against enemy infantry these consisted of wire, anti-personnel mines, MGs, and the indirect fire of mortars and artillery; against enemy tanks there were AI mines and the direct fire of AT guns. Their men were spread very thinly over a very wide frontage, particularly since the defences were arranged in great depth, and the desert terrain was so open – for example, an 8.8cm gun could still do its job even if it was emplaced 2,000 yards behind the very front line.

There was about a battalion (perhaps 500 men) per kilometre of the forward battle zone, which must have meant less than a company (perhaps 120 men) per kilometre in the very front line. Each platoon therefore had to be used to the best possible effect. Rommel's way of achieving this – which he had already applied successfully ever since his first fortification of Halfaya Pass in May 1941 – was to make each platoon position into a self-sufficient stronghold laid out for all-round defence, with plentiful provisions of food, water and ammo to allow it to hold out in case it was cut off. Its communications to the rear were 'hardened' by a network of zig-zag trenches (albeit often very shallow). Rommel also stiffened his Italian allies by placing German detachments at intervals among them, rather than leaving whole sections of his front to be held by Italians on their own. As Eighth Army's chief of intelligence, Brig Williams, graphically put it, there was 'an Italian corset strengthened by German whalebones'.

F1/A: Platoon position including rifle sections, MGs, mortar and AT gun, all located in a 'mine marsh' designed to stop both infantry and tanks.

F1/B: Communication trench, with some rifle pits attached.

F1/C: Main lateral communication/transit trench, including command and back-up facilities for the fighting positions.

F1/D: To the rear of the pictured position there would be another similar position (or several); the long-range AT guns; the field artillery batteries; and ultimately the armour ready to counter-attack.

(Inset 1) The Luftwaffe's Ramcke Parachute Bde – here, an MG 34 crew – were dug in facing Ruweisat Ridge in the centre of Rommel's line, between the Italian 'Bologna' and 'Brescia' infantry divisions.

(Inset 2) Paratroopers bringing ammunition forward up a shallow communication trench.

(Inset 3) GenMaj Ramcke's three battalions of Fallschirmjäger had no transport and were short of heavy weapons. Here they man an Italian 47/32 AT gun – the superior German 5cm gun could not be supplied to every position.

(Inset 4) The unit had its integral light support weapons, like this 8cm mortar.

F2: BRITISH ARTILLERY FIRE MISSION – SECOND ALAMEIN, OCTOBER 1942

Apart from mine clearance, the main antidote to the Axis defences was the creeping artillery barrage: once again, this was essentially a well-tried technique developed in 1916–18, to which Eighth Army reverted after two years of swanning around the desert trying to identify an effective doctrine for mobile warfare. The creeping barrage demanded a large number of well-emplaced and generously supplied guns, and meticulously careful survey, mapping and planning – which could not be improvised in fast-moving encounter battles in some anonymous stretch of desert. It would, however, be used systematically in the set-piece battles from Second Alamein onwards, and most notably at Wadi Akarit on 6 April 1943, where there was a particularly complicated series of creeping barrages. Like all indirect fire – i.e.

As the desert war went on and mines proliferated, the clearance of minefields grew inexorably in importance – see Plate F. Here men of 6th Armd Div are using the basic search method – prodding with bayonets – on the Thala-Kasserine road, Tunisia, on 24 February 1943. Prodding was a slow, nerve-wracking and manpower-intensive method; but although by Second Alamein electronic mine-detectors had arrived and a systematic doctrine had evolved for gapping even the largest minefields, an alert eye and a practised hand for prodding remained an essential first part of the process – as it does even today. (IWM NA 856)

Driver's compartment in a Grant tank – see Plate G insets. The unusual hull design of the M3 Medium made this surprisingly spacious. Note the radio transceiver behind his left shoulder, and his large open front visor. This might seem enviable compared with those of other tanks; but it did let in a lot of blowing sand when on the move, and when closed down for action the driver had to peer through the usual tiny, disorienting vision slit, like that to his left. (Tank Museum 2729/E2)

delivered 'blind' from map references or following the directions of a forward observer – these were devastating to unprotected or inadequately protected troops, and effective against half dug-in artillery (which by its nature could not have overhead cover – although its crews could find safety in slit trenches).

The aim of a 'creeper' was to suppress the enemy ahead of a line of advancing infantry, so that the latter could reach their objectives while their opponents were still cowering and numbed. The barrage consisted of several interlocking lines of continually bursting HE, shrapnel and even smoke shells that would lift forwards at a regular rate – typically, 100 yards every four minutes. In this diagram two field and one medium regiment are firing alternating lines of shells, the two field regiments 50 yards apart, the medium regiment 100 yards apart. This system allowed the infantry following behind to catch up with the nearest line of the barrage to a 'safe' distance (variously quoted, between 100 and 25 yards) before the shells made their next lift. As the infantry advanced they would scour out any enemy positions, theoretically before the occupants felt safe enough to lift their heads above the parapet; and so the offensive would continue.

F2/A: First field artillery regiment (3 batteries of 25-pdrs) lays down its first line of shells at H-hour, c.150 yards ahead of the infantry beginning to advance from their start line. By the time they get within 50–25 yards from it, to 'hug' the barrage, it is ready to make its first lift.

F2/B: First field regiment's fire lifts 100 yards to this line at H+4 minutes.

F2/C: Second field regiment lays down its first line of shells 50 yards ahead of this, at H-hour.

F2/D: First field regiment lifts its fire to here at H+8.

F2/E: Second field regiment lifts its fire to here at H+4.

F2/F: First field regiment lifts its fire to here at H+12.

F2/G: Medium regiment (5.5in guns) lays down its first line of shells at H-hour; second field regiment also lifts its fire to here at H+8.

F2/H: First field regiment lifts its fire to here at H+16.

F2/I: Medium regiment lifts its fire to here at H+4; and second field regiment at H+12.

G: BRITISH ARMOUR IN THE PURSUIT – 5 NOVEMBER 1942

In the pursuit after Second Alamein the British armour was better equipped, not only with the new M4 Sherman but also with Crusaders that had been re-armed with the 6-pdr gun. Both of these had the capability to fire HE as well as AP shells, which should have allowed them to suppress enemy AT guns even without the help of field artillery. However, tank crews had learned caution (or combat weariness) ever since the 'Gazala Gallop' of June 1942, and were reluctant to go it alone in this way. Besides, the provision of field guns in support of tanks in the front line had gradually improved from Gazala onwards, so a viable 'belt and braces' policy was now available, in a way that it had not been in the previous year.

This scene shows a pretty typical skirmish during the pursuit towards Mersa Matruh, as reported on pages 56–59 of Keith Douglas' excellent memoir *From Alamein to Zem Zem* – a journey he made as part of the Sherwood Rangers (Nottinghamshire Yeomanry). This was a notoriously 'horsey-talking' cavalry regiment, which had been mounted less than a year earlier. On 5 November the unit, as part of 8th Armd Bde (10th Armd Div), were temporarily riding 'point' in Eighth Army's vanguard, with one squadron each of 6-pdr Crusaders, Shermans and Grants. They were held up by a light German rearguard, with 8.8cm guns supported by tanks. The landmark of the crash-landed Ju87B Stuka was noted by Douglas as a random example of the debris that littered the North African battlefields. As was increasingly becoming their habit, the British tanks immediately asked the RHA for HE fire from 25-pdrs onto the enemy position. Meanwhile the Crusader squadron ventured forward under fire, but fortunately the enemy guns were hitched up to their halftracks as soon as the shelling started to reach them, and left the battlefield in some haste. Meanwhile a British 6-pdr AT detachment was waiting to come forward and consolidate the ground won. All-arms co-operation had come a long way since 1941. This little 'fireworks day' action may be taken as representative of many others that took place during Eighth Army's hesitant pursuit all the way into Tunisia.

G1: Invisible in the heat-haze, Panzers wait in reserve at a range of 4,000 yards.

G2: 8.8cm guns at a range of 2,000 yards. As they come under 25-pdr artillery fire, they hitch up and withdraw.

G3: Armoured car of 11th Hussars, retiring from its recce mission (it had been shot at by one of the Crusaders).

G4: Two Crusaders of the Sherwood Rangers advance nervously under long-range fire from the 8.8cm guns.

G5: Stuart tank of RHA forward observer, who had arrived to direct the artillery fire.

G6: The Rangers' Sherman squadron follows up over a ridge, preparing to add their own HE to the artillery bombardment of the enemy guns.

G7: 8.8cm air burst: the 'dual-purpose' AA/AT gun actually had a third use, as medium artillery delivering indirect fire. The British themselves would later use a troop of four captured examples in this role.

(Inset 1) The 6-pdr AT gun. It had been used at Gazala, but in inadequate numbers to make much difference to the battle, and its finest moment came in defence of the 'Snipe' position at Second Alamein. Thereafter it became an essential accompaniment to any advance, as immediate consolidation and insurance against enemy counter-attacks.

Replenishment and maintenance was the essential task of tank crews after an exhausting day, occupying hours' more work before they could crawl into their blankets. In this sequence a Grant is being replenished:

(Inset 2) Refuelling from 5gal jerrycans of petrol, while another crewman carries out track maintenance, greasing a rear idler wheel. To refuel a Grant completely meant manhandling about 30 heavy jerrycans.

(Inset 3) Re-ammunitioning with 75mm rounds for the main gun; this meant unpacking and lifting in 48 shells each weighing 20lb.

(Inset 4) Cleaning the bore of the 75mm gun.

H: US TANK DESTROYERS IN DEFENCE – EL GUETTAR, 23 MARCH 1943

(Diagrammatic format, not to scale; each vehicle and gun symbol represents roughly one company or battery.)

The Axis attack at the so-called battle of Kasserine Pass in mid-February 1943 (which really spread to many more places than just Kasserine) had been the first major clash of the war between US and German armoured forces. The Allies eventually won a defensive victory, despite several serious scares. Then, in early March, Rommel had to return to Germany suffering from jaundice and desert sores, and operational command of the Axis forces passed to Gen von Arnim. Soon afterwards the Allies returned to the offensive, and on 22 March the US 1st Inf Div was pushing forward south-east and east from El Guettar in the direction of Gabés. Overnight they were counter-attacked from the south-east by a strong battlegroup of 10th Pz Div commanded by GenLt Freiherr von Broich. He had 57 PzKw II, III and IV tanks, though including only 16 of the PzKw IV

Ausf G with long 7.5cm guns; his infantry rode in a mixture of SdKfz 251 halftracks, captured American M3 halftracks and miscellaneous trucks. His Panzergrenadiers began the battle early on 23 March by opening the eastern section of Route 15 (running east to west Gabés to El Guettar), and securing the flanks.

This plate reconstructs the situation in mid-morning, during the US defence of the heights just to the north and north-west of the main road. Most of the US infantry positions have been bypassed or masked further towards the east, as the main Panzer thrust has driven westwards straight up the road. But just to the west of Hill 336 this slowly-moving 'steel square' (also described variously as an 'iron wall' or 'iron fort') encountered a screen of fire delivered by 601st Tank Destroyer Bn, using a mixture of portee 37mm and halftrack-mounted 75mm guns. There was also fierce resistance from 2/16th Infantry, as well as from 5th (155mm) and 32nd (105mm) Field Artillery battalions. These four units represented a balanced mixture of all arms – infantry, artillery and tank destroyers. The 601st TD Bn's halftrack-mounted 75mm guns were seriously obsolete for taking what was in effect the 'tank' role in a 1943 tank battle; but they 'ducked and dived' in and out of cover, and claimed to have destroyed more AFVs than the 21 halftracks they lost. During a morning of gruelling fighting the Germans were eventually held in check, while additional US forces, including 899th TD Bn with the latest M10 TDs, were fed into the battle. This seemed to be the decisive move; although, like the halftracks, they were vulnerable to airburst shells, their 3in guns were better tank-killers than even the 75mm of the Sherman tank. At about noon the Panzers were forced to retreat some six miles, after both sides had suffered heavy losses.

H1: The initial attack by many of the tanks of Battlegroup von Broich (from Pz Regt 7). At one stage tanks penetrated the US artillery lines.

H2: German mechanized infantry (from II/PzGren Regt 69 & II/PzGren Regt 86) attack uphill on the eastern flank.

H3: Elements of the battlegroup thrust on westwards along their original line of advance, to be halted eventually by 899th TD Battalion.

H4: US 5th Field Arty Bn (155mm)

H5: US 32nd Field Arty Bn (105mm)

H6: 3/16th Infantry

H7: 2/16th Infantry

H8: 601st TD Battalion

H9: 899th TD Battalion

(Inset) Three generations of tank destroyers:

(1) Gun Motor Carriage M6: a Dodge ¾-ton truck with portee mounting for 37mm AT gun – no threat to any medium or heavy Panzer, and vulnerable to all weapons. It was still useful against halftracks and soft-skins, but could only survive on the battlefield by hiding in cover until the enemy came to very close range, and then displacing immediately after firing a couple of rounds.

(2) GMC M3: an M3 halftrack with an awkward, very limited traverse mounting for an M1897 75mm field gun. Again, in the presence of enemy tanks it relied upon mobility and use of cover to survive.

(3) M10 Wolverine: a purpose-built heavy TD with a lightly armoured hull on a Sherman tank chassis, and a powerful 3in (76.2mm) gun in a fully traversing but open-topped turret.

INDEX